Lock & Key

Mental Health: a retrospective review of care and control

M. Rowe

First published 2019

ISBN 978-0-244-49072-0

Contents

Introduction

Having worked as an ASW (Approved Social Worker) I came across much misunderstanding, stigma and prejudice about mental illness generally; and working as a Practice Assessor I found that degree students arriving on placement (third year) were fearful and lacking in knowledge. How to combat this took time and work. As learners, we bring to a new subject some of society's prejudices and inaccuracies, and that takes time and experience to counteract. This book is primarily aimed at those final placement students, who are shortly to graduate, and students on the AMHP course. The qualities and skills needed for mental health social workers and AMHPs are quite specialised. People need to be empathic, organised, up-to-date and knowledgeable about mental health law and be able to communicate with and relate to people who are in crisis. I hope that this book reflects some of the skills and knowledge needed. Added to this is the reality that the law changes, as do theories about mental health. Just about every term or phrase now used relating to mental health is controversial. There is no 'safe' ground. I hope that I have reflected this fact too. At the ends of chapters 2–5 I have referred readers to an interesting article and hope that I have stimulated more questions in people's minds.

Working on a mental health team, either as a student or as a practitioner, requires reflective practice. This book is an attempt to look at real people who are experiencing mental illness and dispel some of the myths around it. We will look at how mental illness affects people's daily lives and how treatment has changed over time. To this end, I have included up-to-date reports (from newspapers etc) written by people living with mental illness, so that the reader can draw comparisons between 'then' and 'now'. There is also some discussion around the Mental Health Act 1983 and its provisions, (applies to England and Wales); a brief history of how the asylums came into being and early mental health law; suicide and parasuicide; inequality and mental health and distress; the possible aetiology of some mental illnesses (depression, bi-polar disorder, post-partum psychosis) and some theories around mental illness/distress.

Mental Health Services are under enormous pressure at present. In this book I have touched on a particular period in the history of the asylums. By the time the hospital at Hatton closed, society had moved on and people understood that such enormous institutions were not the answer to a very complex issue. Unfortunately, the monies made from selling the old hospitals and their grounds were not ring-fenced and invested into what replaced them: 'Community Care'. Mental Health Services remain the 'Cinderella' service, under-resourced and poorly funded. It is easy for us, now, to be critical of the asylum system, and there's plenty to be critical of, but it is important to remember, I think, that people with mental health difficulties can be even more isolated and lonely 'out in the community' than they were in the big asylums.

I have, as far as possible, anonymised the case notes, as requested by Warwick Record Office, and given the patients pseudonyms. Dr John Conolly (a physician from nearby Stratford-upon-Avon) who later became a leading light in the movement for 'moral treatment', helped put together the plans for the building of Hatton, and I would refer you to "Central Hospital Remembered 30th June 1852 – 31st July 1995" (Hunt, *et al.* 1998) for contemporary photographs of staff and the buildings; included is a photograph of the highly respected Dr Parsey. Little remains of the Hospital now, apart from a few buildings, and the records housed at Warwick Record Office.

A very big thank you to Warwick Record Office, Phil Tromans, Jane Burnand, Sue Ainsworth, Dot Owen, Jo Mutlow, Judy Roblin, John Gallagher, Caroline Gallagher and Ian Smith. It's difficult to convey adequately my gratitude to Hannah Davies, Polly Rowe, and most of all to Phil Rowe, without whose help and support, this would have been impossible.

M. Rowe.

Chapter 1

HAROLD

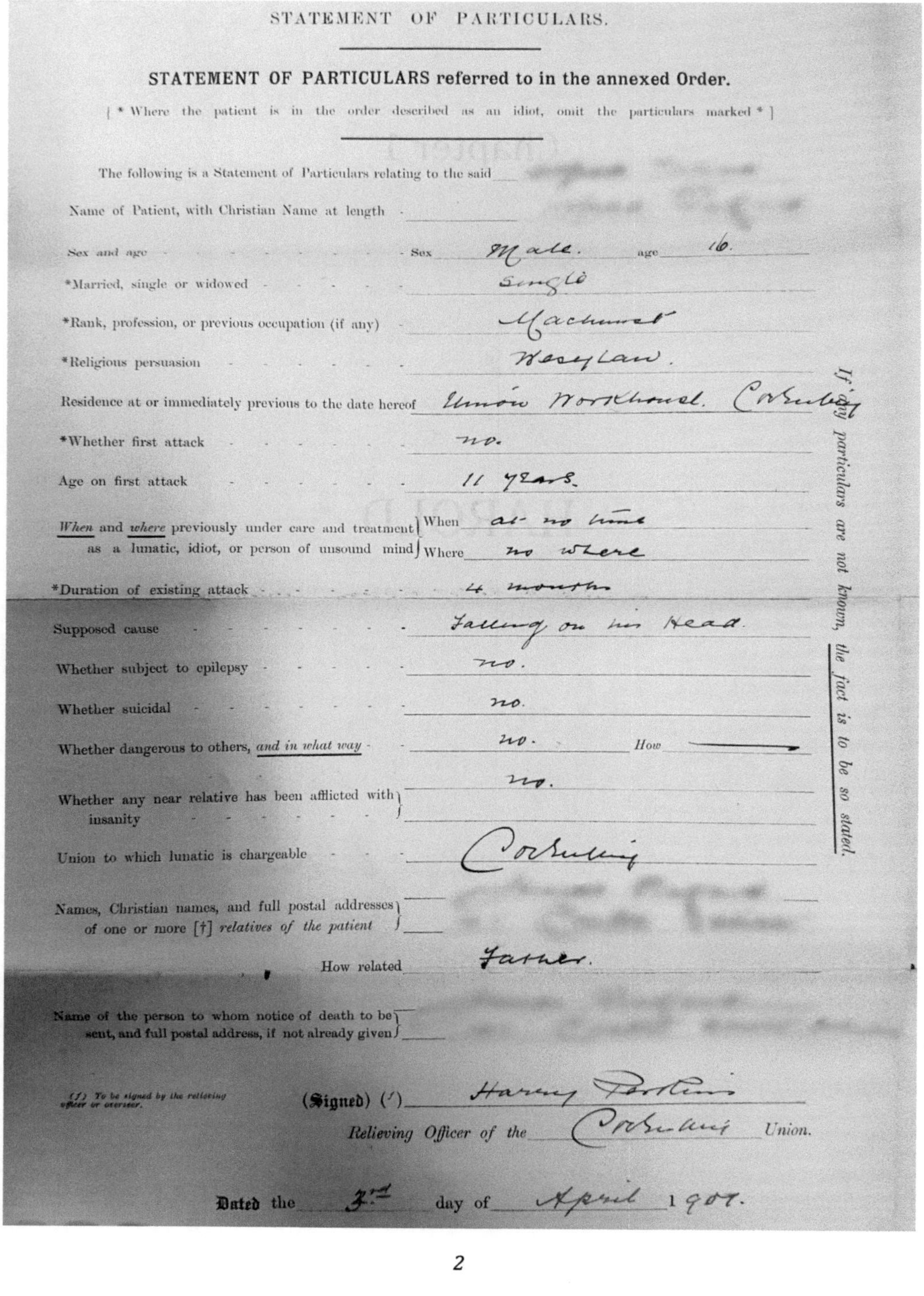

STATEMENT OF PARTICULARS.

STATEMENT OF PARTICULARS referred to in the annexed Order.

[* Where the patient is in the order described as an idiot, omit the particulars marked *]

The following is a Statement of Particulars relating to the said

Name of Patient, with Christian Name at length -

Sex and age - Sex Male. age 16.

*Married, single or widowed - Single

*Rank, profession, or previous occupation (if any) - Machinist

*Religious persuasion - Wesleyan.

Residence at or immediately previous to the date hereof Union Workhouse. Corbridge

*Whether first attack - no.

Age on first attack - 11 years.

When and *where* previously under care and treatment as a lunatic, idiot, or person of unsound mind When at no time / Where no where

*Duration of existing attack - 4 months

Supposed cause - Falling on his Head.

Whether subject to epilepsy - no.

Whether suicidal - no.

Whether dangerous to others, *and in what way* - no. *How* ——→

Whether any near relative has been afflicted with insanity - no.

Union to which lunatic is chargeable - Corbridge

Names, Christian names, and full postal addresses of one or more [†] *relatives of the patient*

How related Father.

Name of the person to whom notice of death to be sent, and full postal address, if not already given

If any particulars are not known, the fact is to be so stated.

(¹) To be signed by the relieving officer or overseer.

(Signed) (¹) Harry Perkins

Relieving Officer of the Corbridge *Union.*

Dated the 3rd day of April 1907.

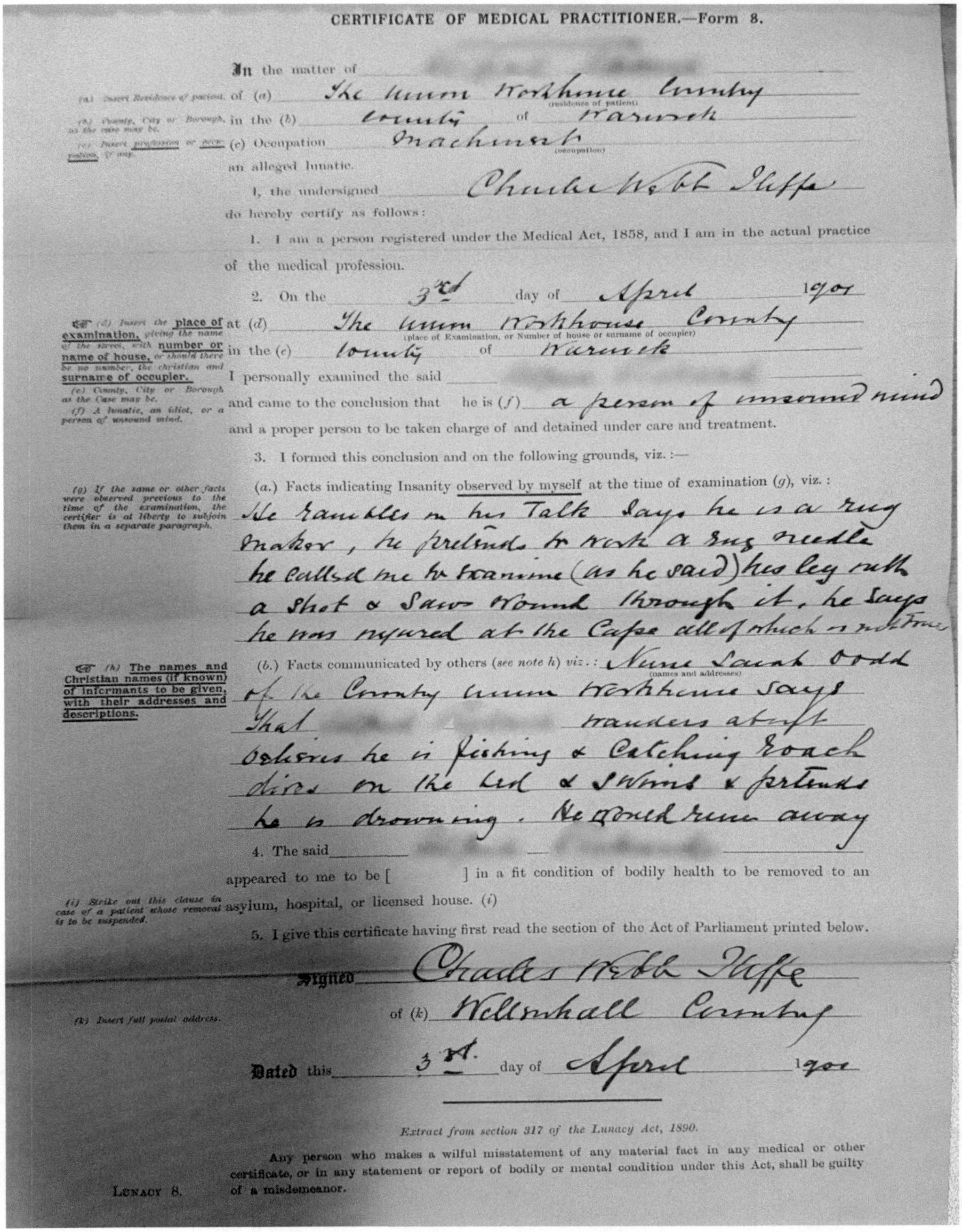

CERTIFICATE OF MEDICAL PRACTITIONER.—Form 8.

In the matter of [illegible]

(a) Insert Residence of patient. of (a) The Union Workhouse Coventry (residence of patient)

(b) County, City or Borough, as the case may be. in the (b) County of Warwick

(c) Insert profession or occupation, if any. (c) Occupation Machinist (occupation)

an alleged lunatic.

I, the undersigned Charles Webb Iliffe

do hereby certify as follows:

1. I am a person registered under the Medical Act, 1858, and I am in the actual practice of the medical profession.

2. On the 3rd day of April 1901

(d) Insert the place of examination, giving the name of the street, with number or name of house, or should there be no number, the christian and surname of occupier. at (d) The Union Workhouse Coventry (place of Examination, or Number of house or surname of occupier)

(e) County, City or Borough as the Case may be. in the (e) County of Warwick

I personally examined the said [illegible]

(f) A lunatic, an idiot, or a person of unsound mind. and came to the conclusion that he is (f) a person of unsound mind

and a proper person to be taken charge of and detained under care and treatment.

3. I formed this conclusion and on the following grounds, viz.:—

(g) If the same or other facts were observed previous to the time of the examination, the certifier is at liberty to subjoin them in a separate paragraph.

(a.) Facts indicating Insanity observed by myself at the time of examination (g), viz.:

He rambles in his Talk says he is a rug maker, he pretends to work a rug needle he called me to examine (as he said) his leg with a Shot & Saw Wound through it, he says he was injured at the Cape all of which is not true

(h) The names and Christian names (if known) of informants to be given, with their addresses and descriptions.

(b.) Facts communicated by others (see note h) viz.: Nurse Sarah Dodd (names and addresses) of the Coventry Union Workhouse says that [illegible] wanders about others he is fishing & catching roach dives on the bed & swims & pretends he is drowning. He would run away

4. The said [illegible]

appeared to me to be [ ] in a fit condition of bodily health to be removed to an

(i) Strike out this clause in case of a patient whose removal is to be suspended. asylum, hospital, or licensed house. (i)

5. I give this certificate having first read the section of the Act of Parliament printed below.

Signed Charles Webb Iliffe

(k) Insert full postal address. of (k) Wellonhall Coventry

Dated this 3rd day of April 1901

Extract from section 317 of the Lunacy Act, 1890.

Any person who makes a wilful misstatement of any material fact in any medical or other certificate, or in any statement or report of bodily or mental condition under this Act, shall be guilty of a misdemeanor.

Lunacy 8.

Opposite and above: Ref: CR 1664/347/1

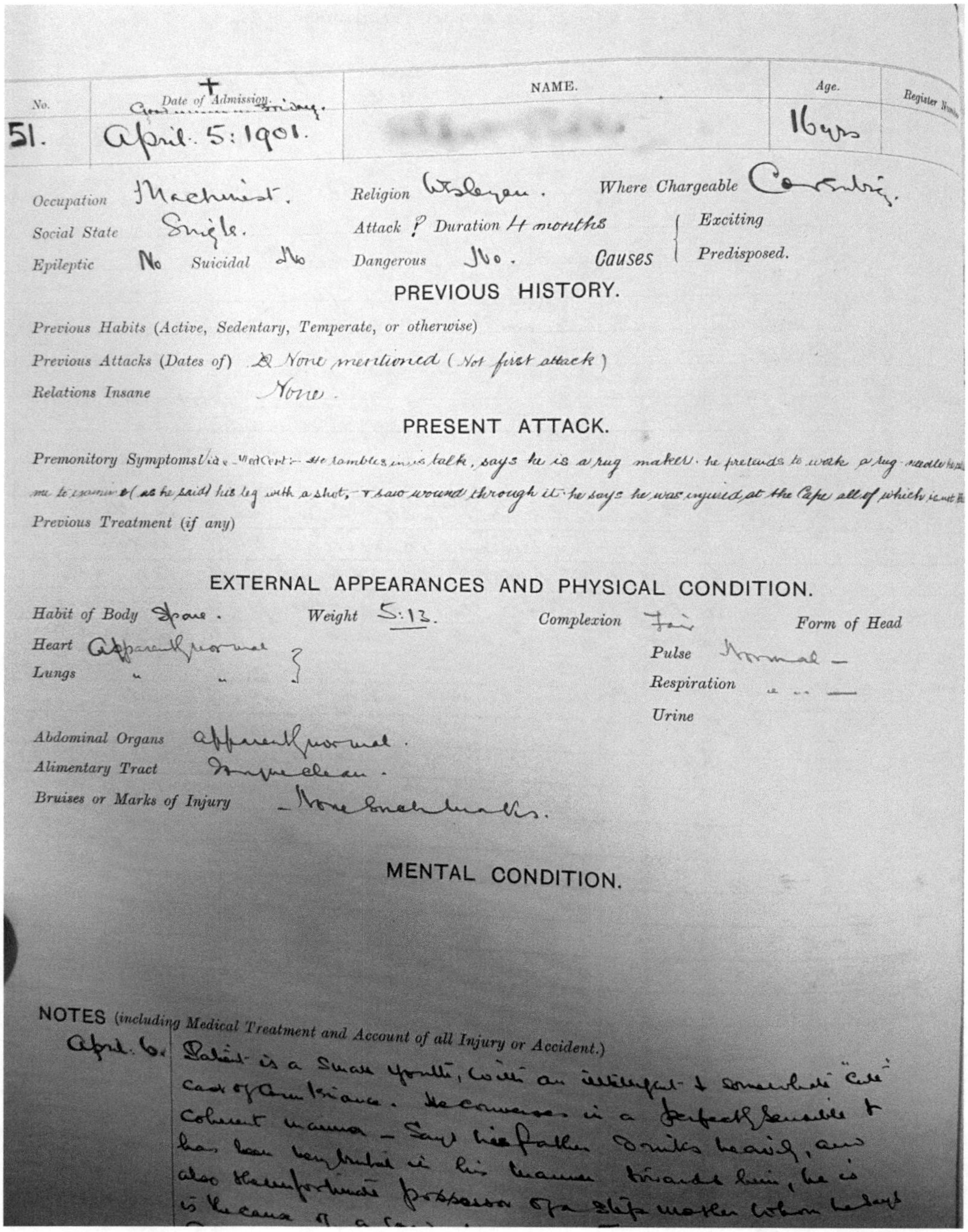

No.	Date of Admission. Good Friday.	NAME.	Age.	Register Number
51.	April. 5: 1901.	[illegible]	16 yrs	

Occupation Machinist. *Religion* Wesleyan. *Where Chargeable* Coventry.
Social State Single. *Attack* ? *Duration* 4 months *Causes* { *Exciting* / *Predisposed.*
Epileptic No *Suicidal* No *Dangerous* No.

PREVIOUS HISTORY.

Previous Habits (Active, Sedentary, Temperate, or otherwise)
Previous Attacks (Dates of) None mentioned (Not first attack)
Relations Insane None.

PRESENT ATTACK.

Premonitory Symptoms Viz. Med Cert:– He rambles in his talk, says he is a rug maker. he pretends to work a rug needle & asked me to examine (as he said) his leg with a shot, & saw wound through it. he says he was injured at the Cape all of which is not true
Previous Treatment (if any)

EXTERNAL APPEARANCES AND PHYSICAL CONDITION.

Habit of Body Spare. *Weight* 5:13. *Complexion* Fair *Form of Head*
Heart Apparently normal } *Pulse* Normal –
Lungs " " } *Respiration* " " –
Urine
Abdominal Organs apparently normal.
Alimentary Tract Tongue clean.
Bruises or Marks of Injury – None Small marks.

MENTAL CONDITION.

NOTES *(including Medical Treatment and Account of all Injury or Accident.)*
April. 6. Patient is a small youth, with an intelligent & somewhat "cute" cast of countenance. He converses in a perfectly sensible & coherent manner – Says his father drinks heavily, and has been very brutal in his manner towards him, he is also the unfortunate possessor of a step mother whom he says is the cause of a [...]

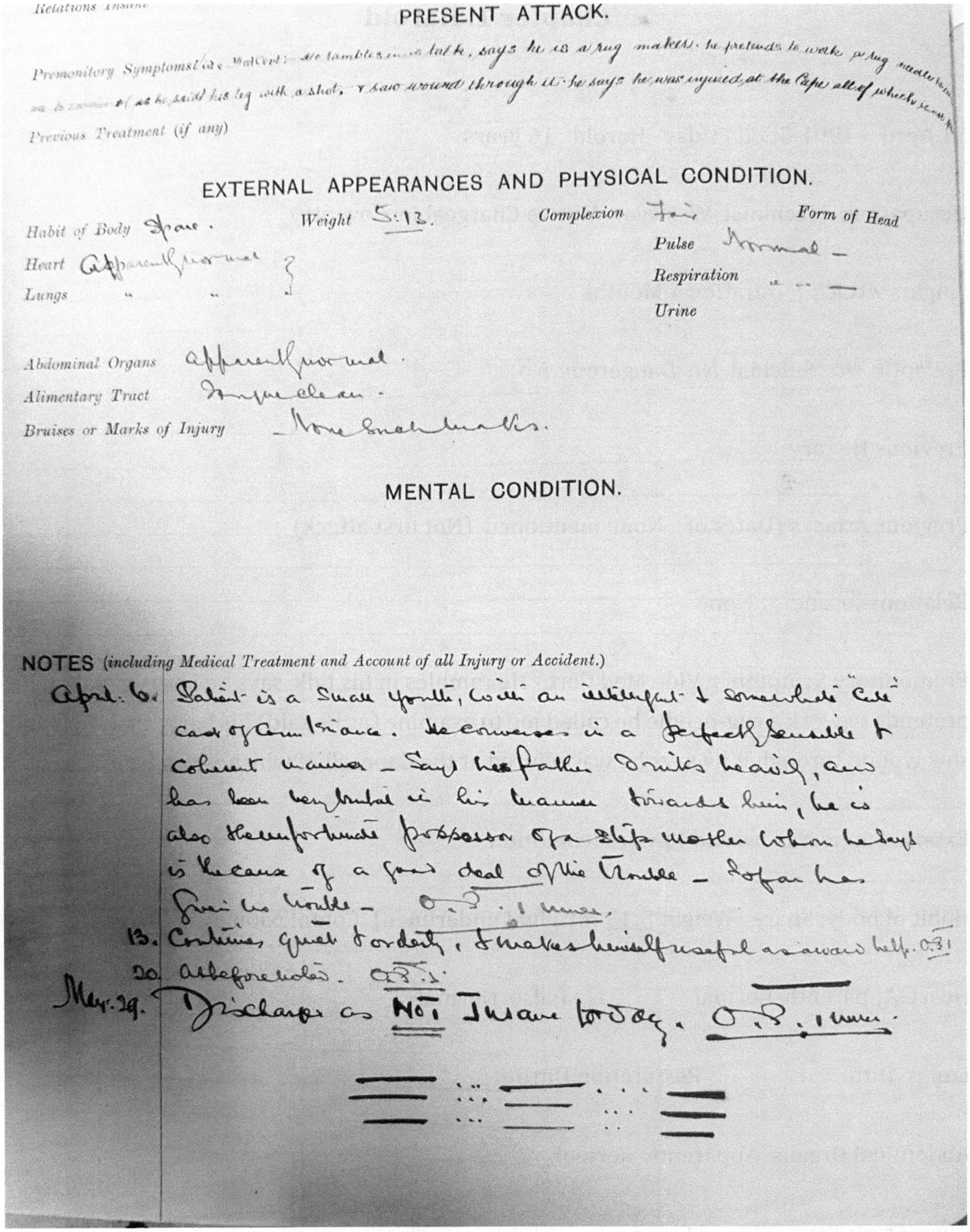

Relations Insane

PRESENT ATTACK.

Premonitory Symptoms (i.e. MedCert) – He rambles in his talk, says he is a rug maker, he pretends to work p[illegible] rug needle [illegible] as to [illegible] of (as he said) his leg with a shot, & saw wound through it, he says he was injured at the Cape all of which [illegible]

Previous Treatment (if any)

EXTERNAL APPEARANCES AND PHYSICAL CONDITION.

Habit of Body Spare. Weight 5:13. Complexion Fair Form of Head

Heart Apparently normal ? Pulse Normal –

Lungs " " Respiration " " –

Urine

Abdominal Organs Apparently normal.

Alimentary Tract Tongue clean.

Bruises or Marks of Injury – None. Snake marks.

MENTAL CONDITION.

NOTES (including Medical Treatment and Account of all Injury or Accident.)

April 6. Patient is a small youth, with an intelligent & somewhat "cute" cast of countenance. He converses in a perfectly sensible & coherent manner – says his father drinks heavily, and has been very brutal in his manner towards him, he is also the unfortunate possessor of a step mother whom he says is the cause of a good deal of the trouble – So far has given no trouble – O.S. [illegible]

13. Continues quiet & orderly, & makes himself useful as a ward help. O.S.

20. As before noted. O.S.

May 29. Discharged as NOT Insane today. O.S. [illegible]

Opposite and above: Ref: CR 1664/639

Chapter 1: Harold

51 April 5 1901 Good Friday Harold 16 years

Occupation: Machinist Wesleyan Where Chargeable: Coventry

Single Attack ? Duration 4 Months

Epileptic No Suicidal No Dangerous No

Previous History

Previous Attacks (Dates of) None mentioned (Not first attack)

Relations Insane None

Premonitory Symptoms: Vide Med Cert:- He rambles in his talk, says he is a rug maker. He pretends to work a rug-needle he called me to examine (as he said) his leg with a shot, and saw wound through it he says he was injured at the Cape, all of which is not true.

External appearances and Physical condition

Habit of body: Spare Weight 5:13 {original underlined} Complexion Fair

Heart Apparently normal Pulse Normal

Lungs Ditto Respiration Ditto

Abdominal Organs Apparently normal

Alimentary Tract Tongue Clean

Bruises or Marks of Injury None such Marks

Mental Condition

Apr 6 Patient is a small youth, with an intelligent and somewhat "cute" cast of countenance. He converses in a perfectly sensible and coherent manner – Says his father drinks heavily, and has been very brutal in his manner towards him, he is also the unfortunate possessor of a step mother whom he says is the cause of a good deal of the trouble – So far has given no trouble.

Apr 13 Continues quiet and orderly, and makes himself useful as a ward help.

Apr 20 As before noted.

May 29 Discharged as NOT Insane today.

The Lunacy Act of 1890 was the legislation in place in 1901. "Vide Med Cert" means that the Medical Certificate has been seen by the authorities at the Hospital, (please see "Admission slip" above). From the admission slip we can glean that Harold was admitted from the Union Workhouse Coventry. Was he distressed at finding himself there and not at home? Was he "faking it" in desperation to get out of the workhouse, thinking that the asylum would be a more comfortable option? We shall never know. We do know that regimes at workhouses were purposefully harsh and punitive (The Poor Law 1832 designed the system to act as a deterrent) and there was considerable stigma attached to being there:

> Conditions for the paupers were only one step removed from prisons – indeed the comparison was often made between the two institutions. Initially the sole advantage that the workhouse had was the inmates were free to come and go more or less as they liked, yet many destitute people preferred to commit petty crimes

> rather than enter the workhouse. It is perhaps little wonder, as the food was dull and meagre, the uniforms uncomfortable, the tasks paupers had to perform were either difficult to achieve or pointless. But above all it was the faceless institutionalism that people objected to: paupers lost their identity (Fowler, 2014, p.102).

As far as Harold knew, there might be no way out of this situation (please see below "Ten Days in a Mad-House" by Nellie Bly). What is clear though, is that after a short period of assessment, the staff realise that Harold is not mentally ill.

So how did the Medical Certificate get written in the first place?

> Since a patient, forcibly removed from the community under a reception order, has a right of action against the person or persons procuring an unlawful removal, it is very important that the legal requirements of the Lunacy Act, 1890, for the completion of medical certificates should be exactly fulfilled. In the main, these requirements are:
>
> 1. Every medical certificate under the Act must be made and signed by a doctor. The statutory form printed in the second schedule to the Act restricts the power to issue certificates to practitioners, being registered under the Medical Act, 1858, who are in actual practice.
>
> 2. Every medical certificate under the Act must be factual – ie, it must state the facts which have led the doctor to form his opinion that the patient is of unsound mind. It is incumbent on the doctor to state both the facts which he himself has observed and the facts which have been told to him by others: reception orders based only on facts communicated by third parties have no validity.

3. Every medical certificate is evidence both of the facts stated therein and of the judgment formed by the doctor in considering those facts. It has the same legal value and effect as if the matters appearing therein had been verified on oath.

4. The doctor must personally examine the patient before writing a medical certificate (Haynes, 1954, pp.509-511).

The Lunacy Act 1890 required the certificate to be made and signed by one doctor. As of 1828, "For pauper patients, only one doctor's certificate was required, with the second being signed by a magistrate, clergyman, school teacher, Poor Law officer or other civic figure." (Wise, 2013, p.xxi). Harold is, for the purposes of the Act, an adult (even though he is only sixteen) and did not require his parents' agreement to be admitted to hospital.

However, abuses did happen. An example of the abuse of certification is cited by Henry R Rollins "Yet another example of the abuse of certification, reported by Dr E Goodall (Lancet, 3 October 1900), is of a girl who 'is a source of great trouble at home, but is neither mad enough to be in an asylum, not bad enough to be in gaol and probably best suited for a reformatory'" (Rollins, 2003, p.293).

> The 1828 Act to Regulate the Care and Treatment of Insane Persons in England (known colloquially as the Madhouse Act) created what the legislators believed was a fail-safe way to protect the sane from incarceration, and the insane from abusive treatment. From now on, two certificates of lunacy were required for private patients, each signed by a different doctor following a separate interview (the interviews to be undertaken within fourteen days of each other); no physician could sign a certificate if he owned, co-owned or was a regular medical attendant at the receiving madhouse (Wise, 2013, p.xxi).

'Private' patients invariably had money, and abuses of certification were often due to financial abuse (dual certification seems to have been an attempt to prevent this). The incarceration of paupers with mental illness seems to have been mostly about social control (perhaps reflected by the fact that only one medical opinion was felt to be required).

Of course, there is a famous novel which includes an abuse of certification – "The Woman in White" by Wilkie Collins. First published in 1859 in serialised form, "The Woman in White" caused a sensation. The novel has a detailed and convoluted plot revolving around the machinations of Sir Percival Glyde and his nefarious friend Count Fosco. They plot to relieve one of the heroines of the book, Lady Glyde (Percival's wife), of her fortune by incarcerating her in an asylum under the alias of a female patient called Anne Catherick. (Anne Catherick and Lady Glyde are physically very similar, being in fact half-sisters; Percival knows that Anne Catherick is an asylum patient because he was responsible for committing her many years before, but she keeps escaping). In the novel, Lady Glyde and Anne Catherick are effectively kidnapped, Anne Catherick dies of a cardiac complaint while in Count Fosco's "care", and Lady Glyde is smoothly "transformed" into "Anne Catherick" the mental patient. Count Fosco relates:

> I took my visitor upstairs into a back room; the two medical gentlemen being there in waiting on the floor beneath, to see the patient, and to give me their certificates. After quieting Lady Glyde by the necessary assurances about her sister, I introduced my friends, separately, to her presence. They performed the formalities of the occasion, briefly, intelligently, conscientiously. I entered the room again, as soon as they had left it; and at once precipitated events by a reference, of the alarming kind, to "Miss Halcombe's" state of health.
>
> Results followed as I had anticipated. Lady Glyde became frightened, and turned faint. For the second time, and the last, I called Science to my assistance. A medicated glass of water, and a medicated bottle of smelling-salts, relieved her of all further

> embarrassment and alarm. Additional applications, later in the evening, procured her the inestimable blessing of a good night's rest. Madame Rubelle arrived in time to preside at Lady Glyde's toilet. Her own clothes were taken away from her at night, and Anne Catherick's were put on her in the morning, with the strictest regard to propriety, by the matronly hands of the good Rubelle. Throughout the day I kept our patient in a state of partially-suspended consciousness, until the dexterous assistance of my medical friends enabled me to procure the necessary order, rather earlier than I had ventured to hope. That evening (the evening of the 27th) Madame Rubelle and I took our revived "Anne Catherick" to the Asylum. She was received, with great surprise – but without suspicion, thanks to the order and certificates, to Percival's letter, to the likeness, to the clothes, and to the patient's own confused mental condition at the time. I returned at once to assist Madame Fosco in the preparations for the burial of the false "Lady Glyde" having the clothes and luggage of the true "Lady Glyde" in my possession. They were afterwards sent to Cumberland by the conveyance which was used for the funeral. I attended the funeral, with becoming dignity, attired in the deepest mourning (Collins, 2008, pp 626–627).

Perhaps what is even more sensational is that although "The Woman in White" is fictional, there are factual accounts of this kind of thing happening, indeed, both Collins and Dickens knew personally that this was so as the Bulwer-Lytton case of 1858 may have been a real-life source for "The Woman in White". What is more,

> In the summer of 1858 three well-publicized cases of alleged improper confinement came to public attention. One was that of a Mrs Turner, a patient in an asylum near York, who was subsequently found to be of sound mind. A second concerned a Mr Ruck, confined in another institution, who was also judged to be

> sane. The third, which proved to be most closely connected with fiction, was that of a young man named Fletcher, a hard-drinking wastrel who claimed £35,000 from his late father's firm. The surviving partners had him pronounced insane and committed to a madhouse, but he escaped and, scenting a sensational topic for a novel, Charles Reade interviewed him. The firsthand information he received from Fletcher served as the basis of a series of letters he sent to the press between August and December on "Our Dark Places" – the unregulated madhouses" (Altick, 1990, pp 45–6).

Looking at Harold's hospital notes now, some things stand out which point not to the need for hospital admission, but for the input of a social worker: he is seriously underweight (there is no mention in the notes of a reluctance to eat, so we may assume that it is not caused by anorexia nervosa); and his description of life at home. Harold is declared not to be mad and disappears from view. What happened to him? According to the 1911 Census, ten years later he is living with his father again and the household has two lodgers (who presumably helped the household income).

Under the law as it is now, Harold would not have been admitted to hospital. Detention under the Mental Health Act 1983 must be a last resort, when all other options have been thought through and discounted. The patient must have a mental disorder of a degree or severity warranting admission *and* pose a risk either to him/herself or others. Part of the AMHP's remit is to think about the other options available in the community (supported accommodation for example) and put those in place if appropriate. In Harold's case, as he is sixteen, a referral to Childcare Services would also be required. None of these options was available in the early 1900s, and Harold would have been sent back to the workhouse. Harold's low bodyweight could be a result of neglect at home, poor diet in the workhouse, disease, or the result of poverty. In our own times, we now have situations developing where people cannot afford to feed their families properly, and the stress of knowing that, as a parent, you are not able to feed your family adequately may well exacerbate (if not directly cause) mental illness:

> More than a million people in the UK experienced destitution in 2015, including 312,000 children, according to a ground-breaking study by Heriot-Watt University academics for the Joseph Rowntree Foundation published last year. It defined destitution in two ways: experience of at least two of six poverty measures over the previous month, including eating fewer than two meals a day for two or more days; or a weekly income after housing costs of £70 for a single adult or £140 for a couple with children. This was an income level below which people "cannot meet their core material needs for basic physiological functioning from their own resources" (Butler, 2017, p.2).

If social work intervention would have been the most appropriate here, why is it that a doctor made all the decisions? The dominance of medicine in the treatment of mental illness has a long and interesting history, and it's important that we understand why, because the dominance remains evident today.

The push to create asylums in Britain began after the emergence of reports of the abuse and neglect of people with mental illness either within their families or in private institutions (like Warburton's houses) or hospitals like the notorious Bethlem Hospital (Bedlam) of the eighteenth century.

> In Warburton's houses, to save trouble and expense, and to allow the attendants some free time at the weekends, patients were placed in cribs at three o'clock on a Saturday afternoon, secured with chains, and left there until Monday morning. In the worst pauper establishments, reformers scarcely exaggerated when they claimed that "fetters and chains, moppings at the morning toilet, irregular meals, want of exercise, the infliction of abusive words, contemptuous names, blows with the fist, or with straps, or with

> keys, formed an almost daily part of the lives of many unprotected beings." Conditions in the public subscription hospitals, such as Bethlem and St Luke's, were scarcely much better. At St Luke's in 1815, there were only sixteen keepers for 300 patients, and the galleries themselves were "overcrowded and cheerless" (Scull, 1993, pp.82–83).

Reform of the treatment of people with mental illness began with the establishment of the Retreat in 1792 at York. The Tuke family (who were Quakers) were the drivers of the opening of the Retreat following the suspicious death of one of their community at the York Asylum. After interest was shown in the practices and care of patients at the Retreat, Samuel Tuke (grandson of the original William Tuke who started the project) published an account of the methods of treatment used there. This eventually led to national attention. These methods became known as "moral treatment":

> it was a general, pragmatic approach which recognized the lunatic's sensibility and acknowledged (albeit in a highly limited and circumscribed sense) his status as a moral subject.... What was seen as perhaps the most striking, both at the time and subsequently, was the insistence on minimizing external, physical coercion – an insistence which has had much to do with the interpretation of moral treatment as unproblematically "kind and "humane" (Scull, 1993, p98).

Oppressive forms of restraint were not allowed ("gyves, chains and manacles") and patients were actively encouraged to find their own means of self-control. Work was an important cornerstone of moral treatment:

> From the beginning of the nineteenth century a gradual process of segregation took place. Poor, able-bodied people (that is, those fit to work) were sent to workhouses, which were orientated towards

> instilling 'proper work habits'. These people were separated from those that could not work, which included those deemed insane and in need of incarceration in asylums. At the same time, ideas about madness were changing. It became recognized as a loss of self-control and not, as previously, a loss of humanity. These changing values were influenced by the exposure of the brutal treatment of those in madhouses. This encouraged the abandonment of mechanical restraints and it endorsed regimes such as the York Retreat (Rogers and Pilgrim, 2014, p.88).

At around the same period of time, came the steady emergence of a new kind of physician – the alienist (psychiatrist). Mental illness obtruded onto the public arena when George III became ill (the generally accepted theory that he suffered from porphyria has recently been called into question (Worsley, 2013, p.1), he may have had bipolar disorder) and a Reverend Dr Francis Willis became involved in his care. George III's physicians were at a loss as to how to cure him and in desperation the government turned to Willis who ran a private mad-house and had acquired a reputation for curing 'nine out of ten' patients in his care. After eleven weeks of treatment in the form of "a mixture of morale boosting and strict discipline" (Jay, 2016, p.60), George was pronounced cured and Willis was famous. George III was at the centre of another high-profile case when

> On 15 May 1800, as he was blowing a kiss to his subjects from the royal box at Drury Lane theatre, a pistol shot missed his head by inches. The would-be assassin was James Hadfield..., a soldier who had sustained sabre wounds to the head while fighting in the British Army against the French in 1794. He had subsequently become mentally unbalanced, fallen under the influence of a Pentecostal preacher and become convinced that the end of the world was at hand. It was revealed to him that he was God's instrument, and by killing the king he would initiate the Second Coming of the Messiah. Hadfield was charged with high treason

> and defended in court by Thomas Erskine, a leading Whig politician and future Lord Chancellor, who accepted the facts of the case but denied the charge of treason... (Jay, 2016, pp.62–63).

Jay goes on to explain that Erskine successfully proved that Hadfield was *non compos mentis* due to the head injury he received while fighting for his country. A medical man was asked to confirm that this was the case, which he did. Hadfield was duly acquitted:

> There was no option but to free Hadfield immediately, which prompted a public outcry and forced Parliament to rush through a new law, the Criminal Lunatics Act, to close the loophole. It gave state madhouses the role of confining 'criminal lunatics' a new class who were excused guilt for their crimes but nevertheless imprisoned for the public good (Jay, 2016, pp.62–63).

This is an important example of the beginning of medical hegemony in psychiatry. As Scull puts it:

> Conditions in the early nineteenth-century asylums consequently provided a promising arena for legislative interference... During this period, certain upper middle-class gentlemen began to interest themselves in projects of social reform of every description... Lunacy reform was soon one of their favourite causes (Scull, 1993, p.83).

Coupled with this appetite for reform came a determined and steady involvement by the doctors of the day:

> At a time when madhouses were acquiring considerable disrepute, Nisbet took pains to emphasise that 'out of thirty-three licences for the metropolis, only three are in the hands of medical men. The chief part is in the hands of persons unacquainted with medicine,

> who take up this branch of medicine as a beneficial pursuit, and whose object is to make the most of it (Scull,1993, pp.208–209).

Dr John Conolly was but one who was involved in ensuring that mental illness became the preserve of the medical profession. This may have been because of the desire on the part of the medical men to attain to the status of a profession and it may also have been societal forces pushing the issue into the arms of professionals principally by the reformers who were largely Evangelical and Benthamite in their leanings. William Tuke at the York Retreat was not a medical man, however, and "moral treatment" was not the preserve of medicine, but what evolved after some time was a consensus that:

> Medical certification of insanity (for private patients only) had been required by the 1874 Madhouse Act as an additional security against improper confinement of the sane, and the doctors now sought to clarify and extend their authority in this area, so as to develop an officially approved monopoly of the right to define {mental} health and illness (Scull, 1993, p.209–210).

By the time we get to 1845 we see Lord Shaftesbury (one of the reformers) presenting two items of legislation to Parliament: the Lunacy Act which placed a duty on all public and private asylums to register for inspection and to have a resident physician (though not necessarily an alienist); and the County Asylums Act obligating every county to build a public asylum. The immediate effect of these two Acts was to rapidly accelerate the numbers of asylums and of those who were detained within them. It is interesting to note that many of the figures who were responsible for the setting up of the original asylums were local magistrates (they were the main people with official duties within local government at the time). If the architecture of the asylums resembles that of the prisons which were being built at the same time, (Worcester Asylum was based on the plans for Pentonville prison, for example) with their galleries and airing courts, perhaps that is why. With time, as the asylums expanded, their architecture became standardised and they housed many people who were the objects of social control. Out of interest, I checked the admission certificates for male patients in 1897 (by this time, the certificate required the doctor to say whether the patient was either "dangerous" or suicidal,) and sixty seven percent were thought to be dangerous/suicidal; in female patients, seventy six percent were thought to be dangerous/suicidal.

As the asylums got bigger, patient care became subsumed to the needs of the institution. Work, one of the cornerstones of "moral treatment" became a foundation of asylum 'care'. At Hatton Asylum, in the Superintendent's Journal, Dr Parsey (trained at King's College London, and an advocate of moral treatment) uses regular weekly criteria to monitor the well-being of his patients to inform both himself and the inspectors: he notes the number of patients in the asylum; the number of patients in useful employment and the number of patients attending chapel (Superintendent's Journal 1858-1869 CR1664/723 Warwick Record Office).

Although Dr John Conolly had made a strong case for asylums to remain comparatively small, economies of scale took over, and many of the asylums became huge (Claybury County Asylum in Essex, for example, housed 2000 patients). The original reformers had believed that an improvement in environment would cure 'pauper lunatics', but as the asylums filled up with more and more people, they became therapeutically stagnant:

> Arlidge's bitter comment on the outcome of reform succinctly summed up the consequences of its central achievement, the creation of vast receptacles for the confinement of those without hope: ... 'a gigantic asylum is a gigantic evil and, figuratively speaking, a manufactory of chronic insanity' (Arlidge, 1859, p.102) (Scull, 1993, p.333).

The asylums became "total institutions" (Goffman,1961,). Hatton Asylum, to which Harold was sent, was one of those built following the Lunacy Act 1845, and Dr John Conolly assisted in the selection of the original plan.

Thinking about the historical background to mental health care explains some of the stigma around mental illness. Hatton Hospital was the County Asylum for Warwickshire, but the vast majority of its patients were paupers who attracted considerable discrimination in Victorian times (hence the Poor Law and the workhouses); the asylums were often built along the lines of prisons; and local magistrates (who also dealt with criminals) were often involved in the building and upkeep of the asylums. Financially better off patients were often sent to private 'madhouses' and therefore attracted less public attention. It was generally believed that the pauper insane were in some way 'defective'; lacking in humanity, lacking in self control. Eugenics fitted in nicely with this idea.

We have an interesting document from America to compare here. In 1887 (fourteen years before Harold was admitted to Hatton), an undercover investigative journalist, working for the New York World newspaper, going by the name of Nellie Bly (her real name was Elizabeth Jane Cochran), managed to get herself admitted to an asylum in New York. Her brief was to:

> chronicle faithfully the experiences I underwent, and when once within the walls of the asylum to find out and describe its inside workings, which are always, so effectually hidden by white-capped nurses, as well as by bolts and bars, from the knowledge of the public (Bly, 1887, p.5).

Bly found appalling conditions at both hospitals she was admitted to – Bellevue and Blackwell's Island Lunatic Asylum. Patients were abused and neglected on a regular basis, the food was inadequate and inedible and patients inadequately clothed. The environment was brutal. Bly is scathing about the 'expertise' of the medical staff in diagnosing her 'madness' and gives plenty of evidence of cruelty and abuse of patients by the nurses. We cannot compare, of course, the conditions at Hatton with those at Blackwell's Island, but several statements in Bly's book feel very likely to apply to any "pauper asylum". When Bly asks for a nightgown to sleep in, she is told by the nurse:

> "You are in a public institution now, and you can't expect to get anything. This is charity, and you should be thankful for what you get" (Bly, 1887, p.52).

On the subject of work, Bly states:

> A scrub-brush factory, a mat factory, and the laundry, are where the mild patients work. They get no recompense for it, but they get hungry over it (Bly, 1887, p.75).

In chapter XV Bly describes the boredom, isolation, fear and despair such a place could generate:

> There is little in the wards to help one pass the time. All the asylum clothing is made by the patients, but the sewing does not employ one's mind. After several months' confinement the thoughts of the busy world grow faint, and all the poor prisoners can do is to sit and ponder over their hopeless fate. In the upper halls a good view is obtained of the passing boats and New York. Often I tried to picture to myself as I looked out between the bars to the lights faintly glimmering in the city, what my feelings would be if I had no one to obtain my release.... I have watched patients stand and gaze longingly toward the city they in all likelihood will never enter again (Bly, 1887, p.73).

Bly describes many "patients" who exhibited no insanity as far as she could see and describes the total lack of rights the patients had to any kind of hearing as to their future. It makes one wonder how Harold felt when he found himself certified in Hatton Asylum.

Under present legislation, a modern-day Harold who is detained has the right to a hearing at a Hospital Managers' Meeting and at a Mental Health Review Tribunal (a court of law held at the hospital at which it is the responsibility of the professionals at the detaining hospital to prove that the patient should not be released). What is more, the hospital managers and local social services are legally obliged to inform the patient about his/her right to a hearing, and hearings will be organised within a set period, whether the patient or her/his Nearest Relative requests one, or not.

At the Hospital Managers' Meeting and the Mental Health Review Tribunal (MHRT) reports are required from the Doctor responsible for the patient's care, the nurse on the ward and the AMHP. The AMHP's responsibility is to provide a report on the patient's social circumstances and how aftercare would be provided in order to enable the patient to settle back into the community, with adequate support, housing, financial means etc. This is partly to provide aftercare to help prevent another spell of illness and time in hospital, and partly to enable those sitting at the judicial hearing to make a sound decision in the patient's best interests. "Sectioning" should be a last resort and people should "come off section" as soon as possible. The decision of the MHRT must be communicated to the patient preferably in person, or to his/her representative. Complaints may be made to the Tribunal office. What is more, the patient, and his/her Nearest Relative (under the meaning of the Act) are given written information at the point of detention, about applying to the Tribunal, about the rights of the Nearest Relative to discharge the patient etc.

> 32.2 The Tribunal is an independent judicial body. Its main purpose is to review the cases of detained, conditionally discharged, and supervised community treatment (SCT) patients under the Act and to direct the discharge of any patients where it thinks it appropriate (Jones, 2011, p.929).

Perhaps the historical hegemony of the medical profession pointed to the need for a professional within the mental health assessment process who was independent and equipped to make a social assessment of the person's situation. When The Mental Health Act 1983 first became law, that professional was the Approved Social Worker (ASW), and at that time the professional independence of the ASW was felt to be important. The ASW's line manager was never going to be a doctor. The Amendment in 2008 opened the role up to some other professions and changed the role title to Approved Mental Health Professional (AMHP):

> The Professional requirements are as follows-
>
> (a) a social worker registered with the General Social Care Council
>
> (b) a first level nurse, registered in Sub-Part 1 of the Nurses' Part of the Register maintained under article 5 of the Nursing and Midwifery Order 2001, with the inclusion of an entry indicating their field of practice is mental health or learning disabilities nursing;
>
> (c) an occupational therapist registered in Part 6 of the Register maintained under article 5 of the Health Professions Order 2001; or
>
> A chartered psychologist who is listed in the British Psychological Society's Register of Chartered Psychologists and who holds a relevant practising certificate issued by that Society (Jones, 2011, p.599).

The work of the AMHP is complex and demanding. Has opening it up to other professionals assisted with recruitment and retaining them?

> A Freedom of Information request to local authorities... highlights a continuing failure to make the AMHP workforce more professionally diverse by bringing in more non social workers, ... Community Care received 102 responses from England's 152 local

> authorities to its FOI. The number of warranted AMHPs ... fell by 2.5%, from 2,174 at 1 April 2016 to 2,120 at 30 September 2017, across the 91 councils which supplied data for both dates (Carson, 2018, p.1).

Uptake of the AMHP role by Occupational Therapists has been low (Knott and Bannigan, 2013, pp.118-126), and by nurses the numbers have been low anecdotally.

> One of the Key Competence Areas (4) demanded of the AMHP is that the applicant has the ability to-
>
> (a) articulate, and demonstrate in practice, the social perspective on mental disorder and mental health needs (Jones, 2011, p.600).

> On the one hand, for those interested predominantly or wholly in *causal* arguments, there is an overwhelming case that past and present social conditions are strong determinants of mental health status. For example, being poor, black, old or a woman alters one's chances at the individual level of well-being, madness or distress. This is also the case when we consider the proven role of childhood neglect and abuse in predicting diagnosed mental disorder. These arguments about social determination can be located strongly in the structuralist and materialist traditions of sociology (especially derived from Marx and Durkheim) (Rogers and Pilgrim, 2014, p.221).

In the notes for Harold, the word "brutal" is used in describing the treatment the boy has been receiving from his alcoholic father. Harold also has a new stepmother to adjust to. The situation at home was likely very difficult. During a Mental Health Act assessment, the AMHP's role would be to look at Harold's social circumstances with a view to assessing the effects his social circumstances are having on his situation. With the cutbacks on services, coupled with a chronic shortage of housing for single people, it might be very difficult to find him support of the kind that he needs, and a modern-day Harold might well find himself either on the streets or "sofa surfing" somewhere.

> Mental Health trusts in England are still having their budgets cut, despite government assurances they would be funded on a par with physical healthcare, figures suggest. Analysis by the King's Fund think tank, seen by the BBC, suggests 40% of the 58 trusts saw budgets cut in 2015-16 (Hutchinson, 2016,p.1).

The importance of the AMHP having local knowledge as to what is (and isn't) available is paramount. The modern-day Harold doesn't need hospitalisation but needs safe accommodation and support.

What are the medical recommendations needed today for a detention under the MHA? (We're just covering the most commonly used Sections of the Mental Health Act here as this is a basic introduction.) Section 2 is usually used for assessment and allows detention in a psychiatric unit for up to twenty-eight days, (necessitating thereby a Mental Health Review Tribunal swiftly after detention). Section 3 allows for detention for up to six months and is used for treatment, and usually is applied for the detention of patients who have an established diagnosis.

Section 12 of the Mental Health Act 1983 gives general provisions as to "medical recommendations":

> One shall be given by a practitioner approved for the purposes of this section by the Secretary of State as having special experience in the diagnoses or treatment of mental disorder; and unless that practitioner has previous acquaintance with the patient, the other such recommendation shall, if practicable, be given by a registered medical practitioner who has such previous acquaintance (Jones, 2011, p.90).

Two medical recommendations are required for Sections 2 and 3. One doctor must have had special psychiatric training under Section 12 ("a Section 12 Doctor") and one doctor should be acquainted with the patient (his/her GP). (It often happens that the Section 12 doctor is also acquainted with the patient, but not always.) The third, and final, recommendation is from the AMHP. Of course, as Harold's case has highlighted, for the detention to be legal, the patient must also be

> suffering from mental disorder of a nature or degree which warrants the detention of the patient in a hospital for assessment (or for assessment followed by medical treatment) for at least a limited period; and he ought to be so detained in the interests of his own health or safety or with a view to the protection of other persons (Jones, 2011, p.26).

This applies to both Sections 2 and 3.

Chapter 2

ARTHUR

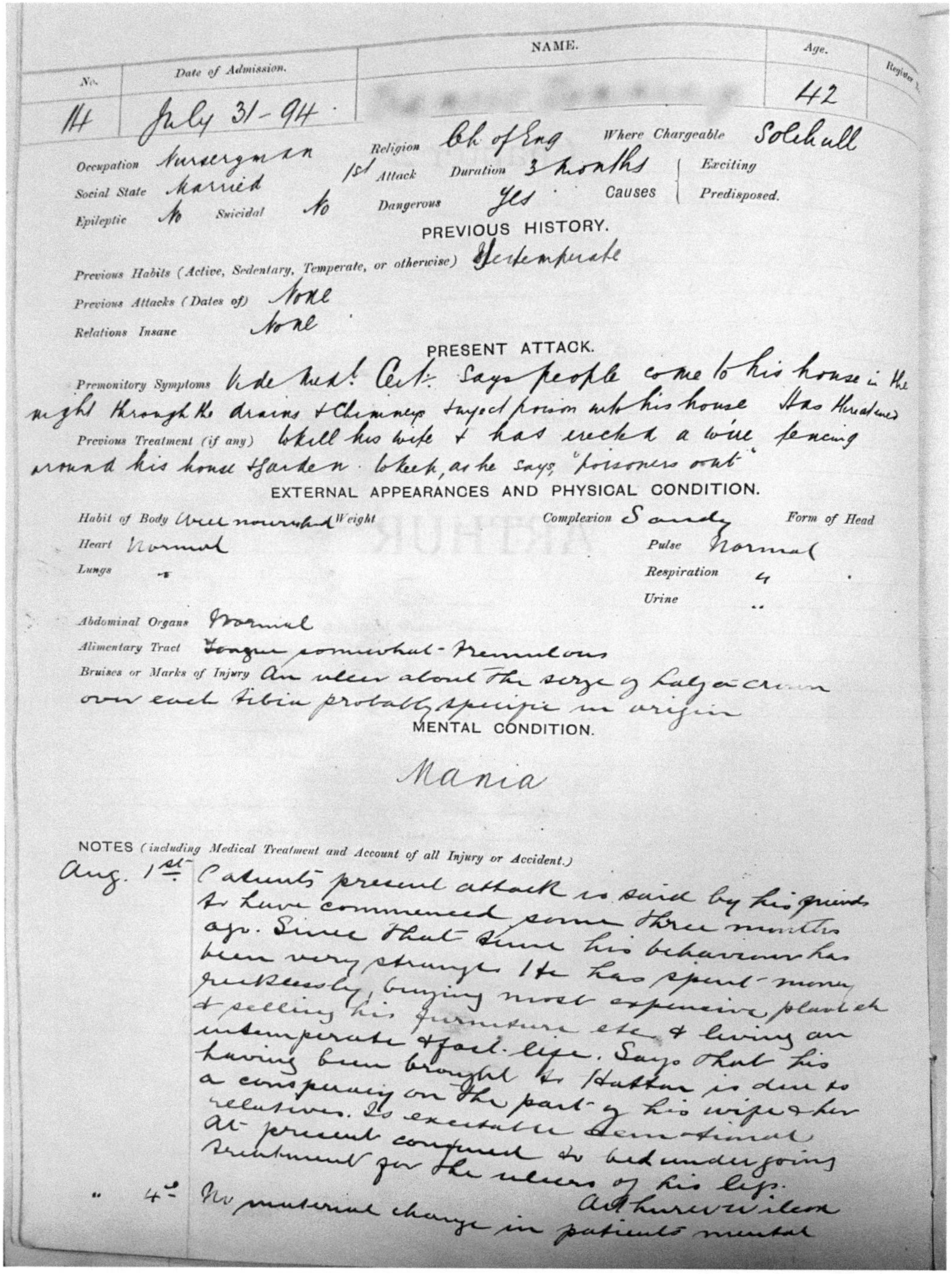

No.	Date of Admission.	NAME.	Age.
114	July 31 - 94	[illegible]	42

Occupation Nurseryman Religion Ch of Eng Where Chargeable Solihull

Social State Married 1st Attack Duration 3 months Causes { Exciting / Predisposed.

Epileptic No Suicidal No Dangerous Yes

PREVIOUS HISTORY.

Previous Habits (Active, Sedentary, Temperate, or otherwise) Intemperate

Previous Attacks (Dates of) None

Relations Insane None

PRESENT ATTACK.

Premonitory Symptoms Vide Med! Cert: Says people come to his house in the night through the drains & chimneys & inject poison into his house. Has threatened

Previous Treatment (if any) to kill his wife & has erected a wire fencing around his house & garden to keep, as he says, "poisoners out"

EXTERNAL APPEARANCES AND PHYSICAL CONDITION.

Habit of Body Well nourished Weight Complexion Sandy Form of Head

Heart Normal Pulse Normal

Lungs " Respiration "

Urine "

Abdominal Organs Normal

Alimentary Tract Tongue somewhat tremulous

Bruises or Marks of Injury An ulcer about the size of half a crown over each tibia probably specific in origin

MENTAL CONDITION.

Mania

NOTES (including Medical Treatment and Account of all Injury or Accident.)

Aug. 1st Patient's present attack is said by his friends to have commenced some three months ago. Since that time his behaviour has been very strange. He has spent money recklessly, buying most expensive plants & selling his furniture etc. & living an intemperate & fast life. Says that his having been brought to Hatton is due to a conspiracy on the part of his wife & her relatives. Is excitable & emotional. At present confined to bed undergoing treatment for the ulcers of his legs.

Arthur Wilcox

" 4th No material change in patient's mental

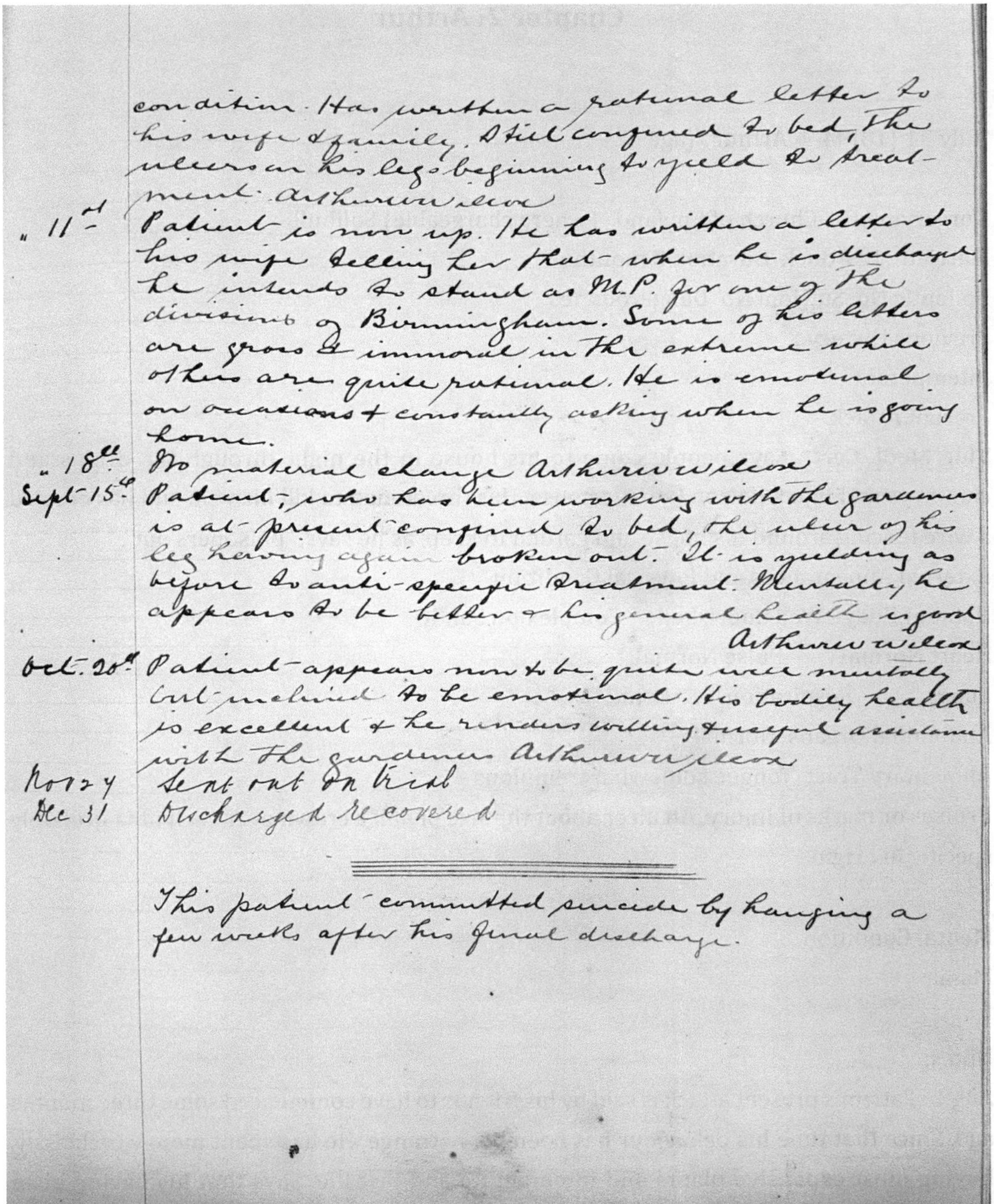

condition. Has written a rational letter to his wife & family. Still confined to bed, the ulcers on his legs beginning to yield to treatment. Arthur W. Wilcox

" 11th Patient is now up. He has written a letter to his wife telling her that when he is discharged he intends to stand as M.P. for one of the divisions of Birmingham. Some of his letters are gross & immoral in the extreme while others are quite rational. He is emotional on occasions & constantly asking when he is going home.

" 18th No material change Arthur W. Wilcox

Sept 15th Patient, who has been working with the gardener is at present confined to bed, the ulcer of his leg having again broken out. It is yielding as before to anti-specific treatment. Mentally he appears to be better & his general health is good Arthur W. Wilcox

Oct. 20th Patient appears now to be quite well mentally but inclined to be emotional. His bodily health is excellent & he renders willing & useful assistance with the gardener Arthur W. Wilcox

Nov 24 Sent out on trial

Dec 31 Discharged recovered

This patient committed suicide by hanging a few weeks after his final discharge.

Opposite and above: Ref: CR 1664/634

Chapter 2: Arthur

"July 31 {18}94 Arthur (age 42)

Nurseryman Church of England (where chargeable) Solihull
Married 1st Attack Duration 3 months
Epileptic No Suicidal No Dangerous Yes
Previous History
Intemperate
Present Attack
Vide Medl. Cert. Says people come to his house in the night through the drains and chimneys and inject poison into his house. Has threatened to kill his wife and has erected a wire fencing around his house and garden to keep, as he says, "poisoners out".
External Appearances and Physical Condition
Habit of Body: Well nourished Complexion Sandy
Heart Normal Pulse Normal
Lungs " Respiration " Urine "
Abdominal Organs Normal
Alimentary Tract Tongue somewhat tremulous
Bruises or marks of Injury An ulcer about the size of half a crown over each tibia probably specific in origin.

Mental Condition
Mania

Notes:
Aug 1st Patient's present attack is said by his friends to have commenced some three months ago. Since that time his behaviour has been very strange. He has spent money recklessly, buying most expensive plants and intemperate and fast life. Says that his having been brought to Hatton is due to a conspiracy on the part of his wife and her relatives. Is excitable and emotional. At present confined to bed undergoing treatment for the ulcers of his legs.

Aug 4th No material change in patient's mental condition. Has written a rational letter to his wife and family. Still confined to bed, the ulcers on his legs beginning to yield to treatment.

11th Patient is now up. He has written a letter to his wife telling her that when he is discharged he intends to stand as MP for one of the divisions of Birmingham. Some of his letters are gross and immoral in the extreme while others are quite rational. He is emotional on occasions and constantly asking when he is going home.

18th No material change.

Sept 15th Patient, who has been working with the gardeners is at present confined to bed, the ulcer of his leg having again broken out. It is yielding as before to anti-specific treatment. Mentally he appears to be better and his general health is good.

Oct 20th Patient appears now to be quite well mentally but inclined to be emotional. His bodily health is excellent and he renders willing and useful assistance with the gardeners.

Nov 27 Sent out on trial.

Dec 31 Discharged recovered.

This patient committed suicide by hanging a few weeks after his final discharge." {my highlighting}

Arthur is exhibiting signs of a mood disorder called Bi-polar affective disorder. Affective disorders are mental illnesses of mood. Bipolar disorder can cause periods of depression and/or periods of mania. Some people swing between the two extremes of mood, some people experience mostly one extreme rather than the other, and some people experience milder symptoms. Arthur is described in the notes as "manic". In a manic episode people experience a kind of euphoria and their mood is (and remains for weeks) inappropriately high:

> The overoptimistic and expansive approach to life engendered prompts pleasure-seeking activities and disinhibited behaviour, which, if thwarted, may provoke responses ranging from irritation to anger. There is a pronounced increase in motor activity, which is goal directed and yet which demonstrates no appreciation of the implications of repercussions of actions... Sleep pattern is disturbed, with an apparent reduced need for prolonged periods of rest. Two or three hours will furnish the individual with limitless energy and unrestrained activity. Social convention and inhibitions are thrown to the wind, as individuals follow their immediate desire, and therefore tactless, offensive and often sexually frank behaviour ensues (Thompson and Mathias, 2003, pp.175–176).

There are signs of nearly all the behaviour described above in the medical notes for Arthur. Unfortunately, people experiencing **any** of the forms of mental disorder, Bi-polar, depression, schizophrenia and personality disorders, are all at greater risk of suicide. In some of the casebooks for Hatton Hospital there are descriptions of manic patients who die of exhaustion because their mania was untreatable and went on for so long. People experiencing Bi-polar Affective Disorder will often experience periods of mania followed by periods of depression, and this is what may have happened to Arthur. The modern-day treatment for Bi-polar often involves taking a mood stabilizing medication and CBT (Cognitive Behavioural Therapy), and an anti-depressant during periods of depression. People are often helped to understand how to avoid triggers and stressors for their illness, and those would be clearly stated on their care plan (Care Programme Approach) and their treatment plan (if they had been detained under s. 3, for example). With after-care and follow-up at home, Arthur might not have taken his own life.

The majority of people who complete suicide are suffering from the opposite mood disorder from mania - depression. What are the symptoms?

They may include: anhedonia (loss of pleasure); feelings of guilt; feelings of self-loathing; increased anxiety; disturbances in sleep pattern (eg early waking or sleeping too much); disturbances in eating (eg loss of appetite or eating too much); suicidal ideation; loss of concentration; repetitious negative thoughts; lack of motivation; feelings of low self-worth; irritability; restlessness; feeling generally slowed down. For a clinical diagnosis of depression to be arrived at, the person must have had these symptoms for at least two weeks. (It is worthwhile comparing the two sets of symptoms for mania and depression: they are the exact opposites of one another.) Depression often, but not always, has anxiety coupled with it, and a useful assessment tool is the Hospital Anxiety and Depression Scale. If used at regular intervals, it will help inform the practitioner as to progress. Depression often follows an adverse event, loss, separation or trauma. (Brown and Harris's (1978) research, for example, shows that children who suffer the loss of their mother before the age of eleven will be more likely to suffer depression in later life.) The most effective treatment for depression involves taking antidepressant medication (and it may mean trying several types before the right one is found) and engaging in talking therapy such as CBT or counselling. Some people have reported an increase in suicidal ideation after starting antidepressants so they should be monitored carefully. Another drawback is that the medication usually takes up to three weeks before good effects are felt. What is more, unfortunately, the risk of suicide may even increase when the antidepressants first start to work, because people who are depressed feel their mood just lift enough to give them the impetus to do something about it. Again, careful monitoring is necessary.

The importance of building rapport and trust when assessing someone who may be suicidal cannot be stressed enough. The interviewer/assessor needs to be non-judgemental and empathic. All the rules about good interviewing apply. Find a quiet, comfortable place where there will be no interruptions (easier said than done on a busy ward in a general hospital, for example.) Allow the person plenty of time (they may be struggling to concentrate, they may be anxious, they may have been repressing their true feelings for a long time). The interviewer may need to ask a series of graded questions starting at a low level leading on to targeted ones. Ask the person if they are feeling suicidal. It's worth noting here that in the historical notes for Arthur, he is assessed as **not** being suicidal. Was he actually asked? (Suicide is, after all, an action that until comparatively recently (1961) was criminalised. Up until that time people were sent to prison after a suicide attempt). People who are experiencing suicidal thoughts may be relieved to be able, at long last, to talk about them. Alternatively, they may find it very difficult. If they are actively planning suicide and have made up their minds to do it they may appear quite calm, collected and not be truthful about their real intentions. That calm exterior may skew your judgement. Remember that it takes time and organisation to complete suicide, people who are actively suicidal will have been thinking about it for some time and making plans.

If the person is actively suicidal and their depression is of a degree that makes their behaviour a real risk and they cannot be kept safe in the community, it may be necessary to detain them under The Mental Health Act 1983. It is most likely that sections 2 or 3 would be used. Section 2 would be appropriate if the person had no previous history of mental illness or had not been detained in the past and allows detention in a psychiatric unit for up to twenty-eight days for assessment (and treatment). Section 3 allows for detention for up to six months and might be used if the patient had been detained for similar reasons before. Unfortunately detaining a person on a psychiatric ward does not automatically make them safe from suicide, and the person may have to be watched around the clock.

There seems to be a marked difference in the statistics for suicide between the genders. "...Men remain around three times more likely to take their own lives than women in the UK and four times in the Republic of Ireland" (Samaritans, 2018, p.7). According to the Samaritans the highest suicide rate in the UK in 2017 was for men aged 45–49; the highest suicide rate in the Republic of Ireland was for men aged 25–34 (with an almost identical rate for men aged 45–54) (Samaritans, 2018, p.1). Unemployment and changes to traditional gender-based roles have left some men feeling worthless and cut loose from the rest of society. What is more, men may feel more inhibited about seeking help for their suicidal feelings and less able to confide in others because of gender based expectations. With regard to completed suicide, they are also more likely to use violent means. The most common suicide method in 2015 was hanging (https://www.ons.gov.uk/).

Men are more likely to use alcohol or drugs in an attempt to cope with stress, and less likely to seek emotional support from friends or a counsellor.

> Men currently in their middle years are the 'buffer' generation – caught between the traditional silent, strong, austere masculinity of their fathers and the more progressive, open and individualistic generation of their sons. They do not know which of these ways of life and masculine cultures to follow. In addition, since the 1970s, several social changes have impacted on personal lives, including rising female employment, increased partnering and departnering and solo living. As a result, men in their middle years are increasingly likely to be living alone, with little or no experience of coping emotionally or seeking help on their own and few supportive relationships to fall back on (Platt, 2017, p.11).

What is more, men, in particular, seem to be vulnerable to suicide when shame and public humiliation are causal factors.

> Honour is also part of masculinity, and to be 'disrespected' in front of others by the actions of their partner (infidelity or abandonment) may lead to shame and/or impulsive reactions, perhaps to punish ex-partners. Men are more likely to be separated from their children and this plays a role in some men's suicides (Platt, 2017, p.11).

Bankruptcy, debt and 'feeling a failure' within the traditional masculine role can all contribute to the risk, and middle-aged men especially, seem to be struggling with the changes in their societal role.

Society is changing. It may be that life is becoming more difficult for some groups who find that their traditional, dominant role is being challenged, (and perhaps a bit better for others (eg women and some minorities like the LGBT community). Is it simply coincidence that suicide amongst women is decreasing? [Anecdotally there seems to be an increase in people being referred to secondary care with anxiety and depression, affective disorders which often have a strong association with social factors.]

Many men feel unable to ask for help because they see it is an 'admission of failure'. This may make the person feel trapped, and feeling trapped seems to be an important factor.

> Specific contexts of adversity where hyper-masculinity is culturally evident (such as in farming communities) has been linked to raised levels of male suicidal action. The usual recourse to hegemonic masculinity in rural areas, serves men well in terms of power and privilege in times of plenty. But it has the reverse effect in contributing to stress in difficult times, such as drought, flooding, crop failure or market downturns. This effect may be compounded by the stoicism typical of rural masculinity, which inhibits help-seeking (Alston and Kent 2008) (Rogers and Pilgrim, 2014, p.42).

Suicide is a complex subject and not all people who attempt suicide are depressed. Some people are more impulsive than others. Some have less social support. Some are struggling to cope with emotionally difficult life events. Some use coping strategies (drugs and alcohol for example) that are unhelpful.

Hopelessness is perhaps the most important risk factor for suicide, and may compound the feeling of being trapped. So important a feature is it, that there is a scale which can be very helpful in assessment ("Beck's Hopelessness and Suicidal Intent Scale"). Hopelessness can, of course, be associated with depression, but there can be "learned helplessness" within families which can be conducive to a feeling of hopelessness without clinical depression being present, just a prevailing attitude (which is, of course, pernicious, and provides the ideal environment for depression to develop). In addition, learned helplessness is often found in individuals who have been brought up in families where problem-solving is inadequate:

> Cognitive dysfunction, especially the mindset of "hopelessness", and difficulties in interpersonal problem solving, are associated with suicidal behaviour. Indeed, hopelessness is more closely correlated to suicide intent than is depression per se and seems to be the key difference between depressed people with suicidal intent and those without (Weishaar & Beck 1990). One implication is that the suicidal person may not in fact desire to harm themselves, but can see no other option owing to the negative mindset in which they are trapped (Thompson and Mathias, 2003, p.395).

Recent research is showing that adverse childhood experiences may have a major impact on future suicidal ideation and behaviour. Recent research published in *The Lancet* looks at

> the harmful effects that adverse childhood experiences (ACEs occurring during childhood or adolescence eg, child maltreatment or exposure to domestic violence) have on health throughout life... Individuals with at least four ACEs were at increased risk of all health outcomes compared with individuals with no ACEs. Associations were... strong for sexual risk taking, mental ill health, and problematic alcohol use..., and strongest for problematic drug use and interpersonal and self-directed violence... We noted an about four-times higher risk in individuals with at least four ACEs across the three indicators of mental distress or disorders... Suicide attempt had the strongest relation with ACEs... Although eradication of ACEs remains aspirational, development of children's personal resilience to enable them to overcome adversity and avoid its harmful effects is crucial. Resilience

> programmes to develop problem solving and coping skills for example, can be delivered universally in schools and tailored to meet the needs of vulnerable children in youth justice, social services, and community settings (Hughes, *et al.* 2018, pp.1–13).

In some families guilt is sometimes used to control members. [It is interesting that guilt feelings (like the feeling of hopelessness) are often present in depression.] Where guilt is used to control others the outcomes can be damaging. As James Gilligan puts it:

> the potential to engage in violent behaviour is built into the very structure and functioning of our central nervous system, which can be "triggered" by the social environment. Unless it is triggered, this potential will remain dormant and quiescent. I believe that the most effective and powerful stimulus of violence in the human species is the experience of shame and humiliation, and that feelings of guilt ... can further alter the resulting psycho-physiological situation, transforming it from one primarily oriented toward the destruction of others into one focusing on the destruction of one's own body (Gilligan, 2000, p.223).

Guilt can lead to self-loathing, which can ultimately result in suicidal behaviours:

> The chief causes of the incapacity for love and joy are *shame* (the lack of self-love, which inhibits love of others, and stimulates hatred toward them and fear of them, instead); and *guilt* (the presence of self-hate, which inhibits self-love, and stimulates fear and condemnation of one's own hostile and destructive impulses and wishes). ...guilt causes, among other things, depression, penance, self-punishment, self-sacrifice, martyrdom, and masochism (Gilligan, 2000, pp.273-274).

> Guilt motivates people to hate themselves, not love themselves, because the feeling of guilt is the feeling that one is guilty and therefore deserves punishment (pain, hate), not reward (pleasure, love) (Gilligan, 2000, p236).

Parenting styles (for example where blame, shame and guilt are used to control) get passed down through the generations and may even lead to a family history of suicide. This history of suicide may add to the risk factor, in that suicide is in some way condoned or normalised.

There have been cases of mass suicide, or suicide clusters, and these clusters are not restricted geographically necessarily because they are 'copycat' suicides, often read about in the media. There was a media 'frenzy' about the incidence of suicide in Bridgend, Wales in 2007/8:

> There are still no official figures but an area {Bridgend, Wales} that would normally see two or three young suicides in a year saw an estimated 25 in two years. All of them died by hanging. A single suicide is an unsolvable mystery. It's impossible to ever finally know the truth; what was in their head; why they did it. In a suicide cluster, this is an unknowability greatly magnified...I outline the coverage to Steven Stack, a sociologist at Wayne State University, Michigan, whose entire career has been spent studying suicide. I tell him about the day-in, day-out banner headlines, the dead memorialised in huge photographs... and he racks his brain... but can't even come up with a near-parallel... But now that the media furore has died down, so have the deaths. Is that a coincidence? And is it just another coincidence that the highest incidence of deaths occurred when the media reporting of the phenomenon was at its height? (Cadwalladr, 2009, p.2–4).

Studies have indicated that portrayals of suicide in the media can not only influence the means of suicide but also increase the suicide rate (Schmidtke & Hafner 1988). This is a major problem

> in devising large scale social prevention programmes that involve use of the media (Thompson and Mathias, 2003, p.393).

Social media may have played an important part in Bridgend. Jean Twenge believes that the smartphone is having a detrimental effect on young people's mental health and increasing the risk of suicide in this group:

> Not only did smartphone use and depression increase in tandem, but time spent online was linked to mental health issues across two different data sets. We found that teens who spent five or more hours a day online were 71% more likely than those who spent less than an hour a day to have at least one suicide risk factor (depression, thinking about suicide, making a suicide plan or attempting suicide). Overall, suicide risk factors rose significantly after two or more hours a day of time online...while conducting research for my book on iGen {the generation of teens born after 1995}, I found that teens now spend much less time interacting with their friends in person. Interacting with people face to face is one of the deepest wellsprings of human happiness; without it, our moods start to suffer and depression often follows. Feeling socially isolated is also one of the major risk factors for suicide (Twenge, 2018, p2).

Social isolation appears to be an extremely negative factor for humans:

> Jean Baker Miller and Irene Stiver, relational-cultural theorists from the Stone Center at Wellesley College, have eloquently captured the extremity of isolation. They write, "We believe that the most terrifying and destructive feeling that a person can experience is psychological isolation... It is a feeling that one is locked out of the possibility of human connection and of being powerless to change the situation. In the extreme, psychological isolation can lead to a sense of hopelessness and desperation.

> People will do almost anything to escape this combination of condemned isolation and powerlessness (Brown, 2012, p.140).

Isolation can be a chicken and egg situation. People experiencing mental illness can become isolated because their normal sources of support may gravitate away for various reasons. In cases like these mental health professionals and social support networks such as MIND can end up trying to fill the gap, and because they are not (and cannot be) synonymous with family or friends, the person in crisis invariably feels the loss. Being a worker in the area of mental health, the ability to form meaningful relationships with people in distress is of paramount importance.

> Low levels of social support *ipso facto* bring increasing social isolation. Social isolation predicts the emergence of mental health problems and relapse in those who have had them in the past. Durkheim's original theorizing about the antecedents of suicide pointed up *inter alia* the integrative and protective impact of marriage, parenthood, religious affiliation and employment. Subsequent research of the ecological wing of the Chicago School of sociology and beyond confirmed that the incidence of mental health problems is correlated directly with social integration (Faris and Dunham 1939, Leighton 1959; Srole et al. 1962) (Rogers and Pilgrim, 2014, p.227).

Isolation means, of course, that the person is not getting alternative frames of reference on their situation (an important component of CBT) and is not getting emotional support. This can also be the case if someone is in an unhappy relationship, of course. Those people (of any age) who live alone, are divorced or widowed are at higher risk. Sometimes revenge plays a part in suicidal thinking following relationship breakdown. Emile Durkheim describes how social isolation can be a factor in the development of "anomie" a possible predisposing factor in suicide:

> Durkheim arrived at a classification of suicide as egoistic, altruistic, anomic or fatalistic. This allowed him to propose, for example, that where "anomie" was a feature of a society – that is, where social regulation through prevailing norms and values was reduced – individuals would tend to become less integrated with society and less protected from suicidal risk (Thompson and Mathias, 2003, p.392).

It could be that middle-aged men are particularly at risk because 'anomie' is now a feature of their generational group. Fortunately, suicide rates for women have steadily reduced over the last fifty years.

Knowing other risk factors for suicide can greatly help during assessment. Other factors which raise the risk:

Imprisonment: people in prison are more at risk, particularly in the first week of their sentence.

Social class and employment: People of social class I (professional people) and people of social class V (unskilled people) and unemployed people are high risk groups. "Charlton et al (1994a) have identified veterinary surgeons, pharmacists, dentists and medical practitioners and farmers as high risk groups. Subsequently, Kelly, Charlton & Jenkins (1995) added farmers' wives to the list." (Thompson and Mathias, 2003, p.394).

> Typically, persons in the lowest socio-economic group have a suicide rate that is about three times the rate of persons in the highest socio-economic group, and the most deprived areas have a suicide rate which is about three times higher than the most affluent areas. The interaction between individual and area-level disadvantage appears to be multiplicative: those in the lowest socio-economic group and living in the most deprived areas are about 10 times more at risk of suicide than those in the most affluent group living in the most affluent areas. Kreitman et al, examining suicide risk in different age, gender and social class combinations, identified the highest risk among males in the

lowest social class in their mid-years (Platt, 2017, p.10).

"To reduce suicide, we need to address inequalities" (Samaritans, 2018, p.7).

Access to means: this follows on from social class and employment, in that people like vets, doctors and dentists have the knowledge and the means to hand, as do farmers (who often own guns).

Severe mental illness: people with a severe mental illness have one of the highest risk factors:

> A seminal study by Barraclough et al (1974) of a hundred cases of suicide indicated a diagnosis of major depression for 70% of the cases, alcoholism for 15% and schizophrenia for 4%. Other researchers have indicated that schizophrenia carries a greater suicide risk than this study suggests, and Miles (1977) and Dorpat & Ripley (1960) have estimated that 10–15% of people with schizophrenia ultimately die by suicide (Thompson and Mathias, 2003, p.394).

When a person is first discharged from the psychiatric ward, there is a substantial rise in risk, as seen in the case of Arthur.

Stigma: It is impossible to overstate the negative impact of stigma in mental illness. Mental illness still carries a great deal of stigma and leads to social exclusion and therefore isolation. Social stigma also has a part to play in the suicides of people who get into debt, or experience other kinds of (public) humiliation. Stigma, of course, results in shame, the emotion which leads to isolation. Unemployment, already a risk factor for suicide, also carries social stigma. Shame can cause someone, who is fortunate enough to have a good support network, to not access it, with tragic results.

Factors that may lower risk:

Close, supportive and confiding relationship;

Religion: may be a protective factor in groups that proscribe suicide, Jews and Roman Catholics, for example.

Life can be extremely difficult and there will be times when everyone will struggle:

> In psychiatry ill health and immaturity are almost synonymous. Treatment, from the psycho-analyst's point of view, aims at enabling maturity to arrive even at a late date... Emotional development starts at an early date, round about the birth date, and leads towards the mature adult. The adult who is mature is able to identify with the environment, and to take part in the establishment, maintenance, and alteration of the environment, and to make this identification without serious sacrifice of personal impulse (Winnicott, 2006, pp.148-149).

Moreover, reaching full maturity may well be a lifelong process, for all of us. People may have experienced multiple adverse childhood events (ACEs) and may develop coping mechanisms which are, in themselves, problematic.

> Among admission to accident and emergency departments for non-fatal self-harm, the majority involve self-poisoning; 10 – 15% tend to be cases of self-injury, with most of these involving cutting (Hawton & Catalan 1987). Many admissions are of people who have harmed themselves before and whose problem has therefore not been successfully addressed. Some of these people will go on to actually kill themselves (Hawton & Fagg 1988) (Thompson and Mathias, 2003, p.390).

It needs to be understood that some adults and children have had the misfortune to experience levels of abuse and neglect that nothing could prepare them for, and that it may take many years of therapy and treatment before they arrive at a point where they can 'identify with the environment' and take part in some kind of satisfying life.

Such situations as outlined above are probably more aligned with deliberate self-harm (DSH) than suicide, and sometimes given the label "parasuicide". Sometimes alcohol plays a part. People turn to alcohol as a coping mechanism, but it becomes an aggravating factor: alcohol has the effect of increasing people's impulsivity and affecting their judgement deleteriously. An unfortunately common scenario is when a relationship break-up becomes the background for an over-dose of alcohol (which is also a depressant) followed by an over-dose of (typically) paracetamol.

In the article quoted at the end of this section, ambivalence is cited as a major factor in suicide, and this seems correct. At the time of the overdose, in such situations described as parasuicide, people often take the overdose impulsively and then regret it. Winnicott's concept of the 'false self' might help us to understand some kinds of DSH:

> The false self is built up on a basis of compliance. It can have a defensive function, which is the protection of the true self...only the true self can feel real, but the true self must never be affected by external reality, must never comply. When the false self becomes exploited and treated as real there is a growing sense in the individual of futility and despair. Naturally in individual life there are all degrees of this state of affairs so that commonly the true self is protected but has some life and the false self is the social attitude. At the extreme of abnormality the false self can easily get itself mistaken for real, so that the real self is under threat of annihilation; suicide can then be a reassertion of the true self (Winnicott, 2007, p.133).

Winnicott goes on to explain how the false self evolves (Winnicott, 2007, p.145) and his theory could be important in helping us to understand repeated DSH and some of the ambivalence that often accompanies it. In very simple terms, Winnicott's theory is that at a time before the baby understands itself to be a separate entity from her/his mother, "the good enough mother" mirrors her baby's gestures and responds to them, rather than expecting the baby to respond to her. This sensitive care allows the baby's own personality (rather than a "false self") to develop. 'Love' is essential for the baby's survival, of course, and the baby will love her/his parents, whatever the quality of the parenting, because her/his survival depends upon it. According to this theory, the adult who repeatedly attempts suicide is trying to annihilate the false self which is causing them feelings of despair and hopelessness, but that means, of course, annihilating the true self too. Destruction of the false self would bring relief, but it would also involve the destruction of the true self, the self the person is trying to reach – hence the ambivalence.

In a very real sense, though, each suicide happens to a unique person with a unique set of circumstances. The risk factors outlined above can only be guidelines, parameters when assessing that individual person in crisis.

> **"How to get to a world without suicide**
>
> After his son's suicide aged 18, Steve Mallen sees the world differently. Along with a growing number of mental health experts, he wants to reduce the rate of suicide across the world, and is aiming for zero" (Usborne, 2017) https://www.theguardian.com/society/2017/aug/01/zero-suicide-the-bold-new-fight-to-eradicate-suicide?

Chapter 3

EDITH

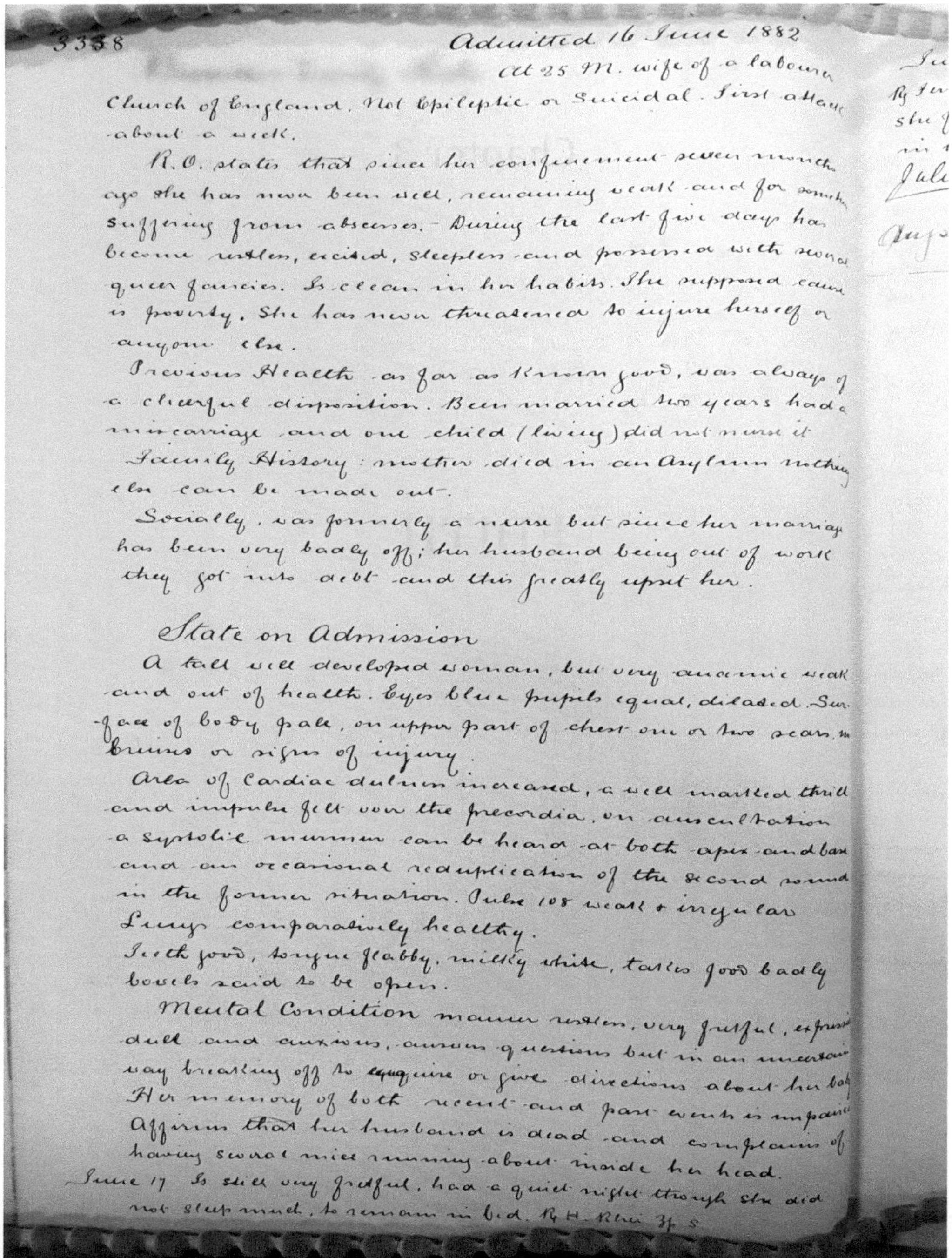

3338 Admitted 16 June 1882

Æt 25 M. wife of a labourer

Church of England, Not Epileptic or Suicidal. First attack about a week.

R.O. states that since her confinement seven months ago she has never been well, remaining weak and for some time suffering from abscesses. During the last five days has become restless, excited, sleepless and possessed with several queer fancies. Is clean in her habits. The supposed cause is poverty. She has never threatened to injure herself or anyone else.

Previous Health as far as known good, was always of a cheerful disposition. Been married two years had a miscarriage and one child (living) did not nurse it.

Family History: mother died in an Asylum nothing else can be made out.

Socially, was formerly a nurse but since her marriage has been very badly off; her husband being out of work they got into debt and this greatly upset her.

State on Admission

A tall well developed woman, but very anaemic weak and out of health. Eyes blue pupils equal, dilated. Surface of body pale, on upper part of chest one or two scars, no bruises or signs of injury.

Area of Cardiac dulness increased, a well marked thrill and impulse felt over the precordia, on auscultation a systolic murmur can be heard at both apex and base and an occasional reduplication of the second sound in the former situation. Pulse 108 weak & irregular

Lungs comparatively healthy.

Teeth good, tongue flabby, milky white, takes food badly bowels said to be open.

Mental Condition manner restless, very fretful, expression dull and anxious, answers questions but in an uncertain way breaking off to enquire or give directions about her baby. Her memory of both recent and past events is impaired. Affirms that her husband is dead and complains of having several mice running about inside her head.

June 17 Is still very fretful, had a quiet night though she did not sleep much, to remain in bed. Rx H. Rhei ʒj s.

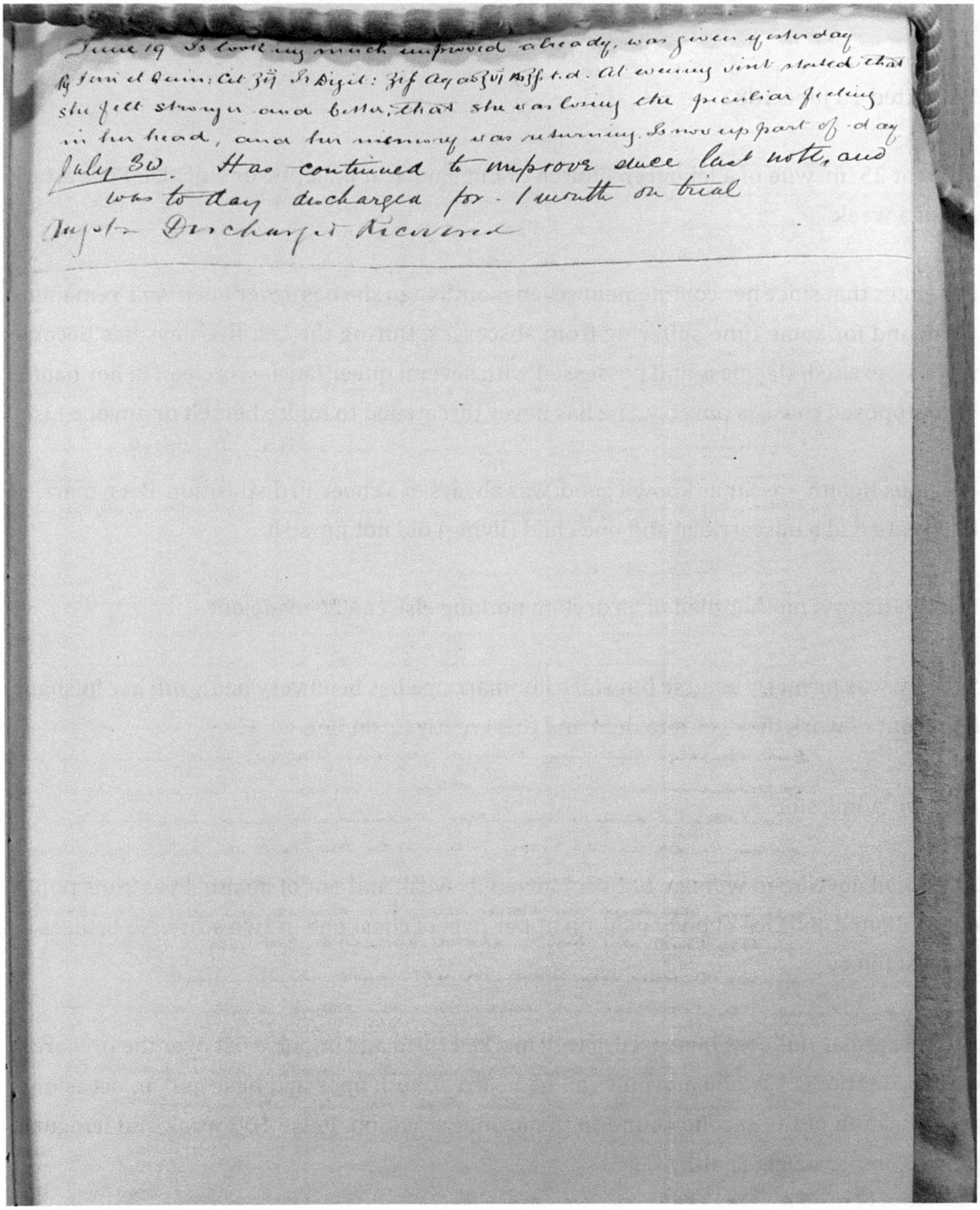

June 19 Is looking much improved already, was given yesterday
R Ferri et Quin: Cit ℨiij Tr Digit: ℨif Aq ad ℥vj ℨss t.d. At evening visit stated that
she felt stronger and better, that she was losing the peculiar feeling
in her head, and her memory was returning. Is now up part of day
July 30. Has continued to improve since last note, and
was to day discharged for 1 month on trial
Augst Discharged Recovered

Opposite and above: Ref: CR 1664/652

Chapter 3: Edith

"Admitted 16 June 1882

Edith at 25 m. wife of a labourer. Church of England. Not epileptic or suicidal. First attack about a week.

R.O states that since her confinement seven months ago she has never been well, remaining weak and for some time suffering from abscesses. During the last five days has become restless, excited, sleepless and possessed with several queer fancies. Is clean in her habits. The supposed cause is poverty. She has never threatened to injure herself or anyone else.

Previous Health – as far as known good, was always of a cheerful disposition. Been married two years had a miscarriage and one child (living) did not nurse it.

Family History: mother died in an asylum nothing else can be made out.

Socially, was formerly a nurse but since her marriage has been very badly off; her husband being out of work they got into debt and this greatly upset her.

State on Admission

A tall well developed woman, but very anaemic, weak and out of health. Eyes blue, pupils equal, dilated. Surface of body pale, on upper part of chest one or two scars. No bruises or signs of injury.

Area of cardiac dullness increased, a well marked thrill and impulse felt over the precordia on auscultation a systolic murmur can be heard at both apex and base and an occasional reduplication of the second sound in the former situation. Pulse 108 weak and irregular. Lungs comparatively healthy.

Teeth good, tongue flabby, milky white, takes food badly, bowels said to be open.

Mental Condition: Manner restless, very fretful, expression dull and anxious, answers questions but in an uncertain way breaking off to enquire or give directions about her baby. Her memory of both recent and past events is ? unprecise. Affirms that her husband is dead and complains of having several mice running about inside her head.

June 17 Is still very fretful, had a quiet night though she did not sleep much, to remain in bed. R H Rheu 3p S.

June 19 Is looking much improved already, was given yesterday Rg Ferri et Quin Cit 3" Digit t.d.

At evening visit stated that she felt stronger and better, that she was losing the peculiar feeling in her head, and her memory was returning. Is now up part of the day.

July 30 Has continued to improve since last note, and was today discharged for 1 month on trial.

August – Discharged Recovered."

We know from the Census records that Edith gave birth to a male child (Y) on 14th December 1881. On 15th February 1883 Edith had another baby boy (Z) and he was also born in Warwickshire. Sadly, in October 1883 Z dies in Prescot, Lancashire. The family seems to have moved to Lancashire in 1883, probably in search of work. By the time the 1891 Census was taken the family were living in Widnes, Lancashire. Their eldest son is still living and they also have X (born in Widnes, in about 1890). The family have two apprentice labourers living with them as boarders. We don't know what caused Z's death, but it could well have been poverty.

Edith was admitted to hospital because she was suffering a physical illness. Modern medical opinion of the notes suggests that Edith was suffering from Atrial Fibrillation, almost certainly as a result of Rheumatic heart disease. The Ferri et Quin Cit is an iron mixture (given for anaemia) and the Digit is digitalis mixture to treat the Atrial Fibrillation. The treatment makes sound sense and explains Edith's good recovery. The doctor treating Edith is quite clear that her admission is due to poverty. She had not been nursing her baby, so Edith's illness is not attributable to "milk fever" (exhaustion and anaemia), another common cause of admission at the time, where impoverished women, often on poor diets, continued to breast feed their children to the detriment of their own health because it saved money and helped to prevent pregnancy. There was, after all, no pre- or post-natal care, no follow-up, no benefits, no contraceptive advice and the family was in debt with no money coming in. A modern-day Edith would be entitled to certain benefits whilst pregnant and during the first twelve months after the birth of her child. She would also be entitled to free prescriptions and dental care on the NHS for that period (National Health Service, 2019).

The family would have struggled on a farm labourer's wages. Farm labour was poorly paid and the work was patchy with not much available in the winter. Indeed, the plight of farm labourers was one of the drivers behind the Poor Law Act of 1832 – so many of the rural poor were needing "outdoor relief". Prior to 1832, the poor had been helped in times of need with, for example, a bag of coal, or loaves of bread paid for through local taxes and distributed by local officials called Overseers of the Poor, but after 1832 this was expressly discouraged and poor people were told that if they could not manage in the community, they must enter the workhouse, where conditions were made as unpleasant as possible as a deterrent (one is tempted to say punishment). It wasn't just the rural poor who were struggling either, "Low pay was a significant cause of London poverty throughout the century. The figures are uncertain but Booth thought at least a sixth of family poverty was due to wages too low to live on" (White, 2008, p 180).

It's worth noting here that gender discrimination in Victorian society would have increased the numbers of poor women who were admitted to the workhouse and asylum. Working class women were often forced into the lowest paid, most menial and degrading jobs (household servants, launderesses, governesses). As a consequence, they received lower wages than their male counterparts (as did the female attendants and Matron at Hatton Hospital) and were generally poorer than men. Women were thought to be more prone to mental illness, but was this, in actual fact, a reflection of their place in society? (Ironically, the gender pay gap remains very much alive and kicking to the present day.)

In the modern day, someone experiencing a physical illness (like Edith), would not be admitted to a psychiatric unit. It is part of the assessing doctors' remit to think carefully as to whether the person's symptoms could be caused by a physical as opposed to a mental illness.

What I hope to show in this chapter is that inequality is a bad thing in itself. That sounds very obvious, but it seems to be something that society hasn't learned. It is well known that people with low incomes have poorer outcomes for their physical health and die earlier than those with higher incomes, but what about their mental health? And what about the outcomes for children, like Y, born into poor families? There is a very real possibility that government policy is pushing people back into poverty (in order to 'incentivise' them to work) and may have the opposite effect, and simply set up a vicious cycle of deprivation, poor physical and mental health and perpetuate the need for benefit payment and costly health spending in the future. The danger is that inequality will adversely affect the mental health of children, and society will be storing up problems for the future which may be even more expensive to redress, this quite apart from the individual suffering inequality causes.

With regard to mental health, we have seen elsewhere in this book how the emotions of shame and guilt can affect people, and Gilligan has more to say about the effect of shame on poor people:

> John Adams, writing two centuries ago, noticed that the condition of poverty exposed the poor to shame, not guilt. As he described the situation, "The poor man's conscience is clear" – i.e., he does not feel guilty, and has no reason to – "yet he is ashamed." Why is this? ... "Mankind takes no notice of him. He rambles and wanders unheeded. In the midst of a crowd; at church; in the market ... he

> is in as much obscurity as he would be in a garret or a cellar. He is not disapproved, censured, or reproached; he is only not seen. To be wholly overlooked, and to know it, are intolerable (Gilligan, 2000, p.198).

It should be added here, that good self-esteem is a corner-stone of good mental health, and if financial inequality is one jeopardy that can affect people's mental health, then we should also look at the other potential jeopardies which multiply the risk – gender inequality, sexual discrimination, and racism. I failed to find a patient with a BAME background in the Hatton hospital records, so instead of dedicating a chapter to discrimination on racial terms, I shall discuss some of the risks associated with racial discrimination here: for example, "black men were more than 10 times as likely to have experienced a psychotic disorder within the past year as white men" (Mulholland,2017, p.3). According to the Mental Health Bulletin,

> nearly 5000 "black" or "black British" people per 100,000 accessed mental health services in 2014 – 2015; 12.7% of those in contact with mental health and learning disability services spent at least one night in hospital that year. That's more than double the percentage in the white population (Ferguson, 2016, p.1).

In a newspaper article about inequality, some of the black women interviewed state that they feel that they cannot be themselves in British society:

> "I have to prove that I can do the same thing as a white person", messaged Naomi, who is 31 and works as a marketing executive in the city. "Often what I say will be ignored, then someone who is not black will say it and all of a sudden it makes sense!" (Ferguson, 2016, p.2).

What Naomi is describing here is described by Gilligan as 'slighting' or undermining, which is a component of racism and has a detrimental effect on self-esteem over time, and causes stress, one of the likely triggers for mental illness:

$$\text{Incidence of mental illness} = \frac{\text{stress + exploitation + organic factors}}{\text{support + self-esteem + coping skills}}$$

Figure 13.1 Distinguishing the incidence of mental illness from the promotion of mental health using common factors (modified from Albee (1993). (Rogers and Pilgrim, 2014, p 222).

The effects of racism, poverty, sexism are all factors in developing mental distress, but what are the causes of racism? There is no scientific, genetic factuality to racism. Toni Morrison looks at racism and its evolution and effects in "The Origin of Others". In the Foreword by Ta-Nehisi Coates, he writes:

> When we say "race" as opposed to "racism", we reify the idea that race is somehow a feature of the natural world and racism the predictable result of it. Despite the body of scholarship that has accumulated to show that this formulation is backwards, that racism precedes race, Americans still haven't quite gotten the point. And so we find ourselves speaking of "racial segregation," "the racial chasm", "the racial divide", "racial profiling", or "racial diversity" – as though each of these ideas is grounded in something beyond our own making. The impact of this is not insignificant. If "race" is the work of genes or gods, or both, then we can forgive ourselves for never having unworked the problem (Morrison, 2017, p.xi).

Morrison goes on, in the main body of the book, to look at the origins of "Otherness":

> We are aware of strategies for survival in the natural world: distraction/sacrifice to protect the nest; pack hunting/chasing food on the hoof. But for humans as an advanced species, our tendency to separate and judge those not in our clan as the enemy, as the vulnerable and the deficient needing control, has a long history not limited to the animal world or prehistoric man. Race has been a constant arbiter of difference, as have wealth, class, and gender – each of which is about power and the necessity to control (Morrison, 2017, p.3).

Morrison calls this human tendency to discriminate against 'those not in our clan' as 'othering' and asks:

> What is the nature of Othering's comfort, its allure, its power (social, psychological, or economical)? Is it the thrill of belonging – which implies being part of something bigger than one's solo self, and therefore stronger? My initial view leans toward the social/psychological need for a "stranger", an Other in order to define the estranged self (the crowd seeker is always the lonely one) (Morrison, 2017, p.15).

In the descriptions Morrison gives of the inhuman behaviour of the slave owners towards their slaves ("How hard they work to define the slave as inhuman, savage, when in fact the definition of the inhuman describes overwhelmingly the punisher" (Morrison, 2017, p.29)) is a good example of projection:

> It's as though they are shouting, "I am not a beast! I'm not a beast! I torture the helpless to prove I am not weak." The danger of sympathizing with the stranger is the possibility of becoming a stranger. To lose one's racial-ized rank is to lose one's own valued and enshrined difference (Morrison, 2017, p.30).

Morrison goes on to say:

> It took some time for me to understand... that there are no strangers. There are only versions of ourselves, many of which we have not embraced, most of which we wish to protect ourselves from. For the stranger is not foreign, she is random; not alien but remembered; and it is the randomness of the encounter with our already known – although unacknowledged – selves that summons a ripple of alarm. That makes us reject the figure and the emotions it provokes – especially when these emotions are profound. It is also what makes us want to own, govern, and administrate the Other. To romance her, if we can, back into our own mirrors. In either instance (of alarm or false reverence), we deny her personhood, the specific individuality we insist upon for ourselves (Morrison, 2017, p.38).

The understanding of the formulation of the Other is extremely pertinent to both social care and mental health care, and also explains how stigma comes about. Our institutions are but small reflections of the bigger mirror of society. In an unequal society where the white, male, sane, heterosexual and wealthy dominate, large numbers of people who do not fit those criteria will struggle and many are actively discriminated against, stigmatised, or made invisible and unheard. Although societal changes have improved the situation for the LGBT community, we still have a long way to go to counteract the discrimination they still face:

> New research from Stonewall, Britain's leading charity for lesbian, gay, bi and trans equality, exposes alarming levels of poor mental health among LGBT people compared to the general population. Stonewall's study also reveals a shockingly high level of hostility and unfair treatment by many LGBT people when accessing healthcare services... Half of LGBT people (52 per cent) have experienced depression, while three in five (61 per cent) reported

> having episodes of anxiety. And it's no wonder this is the case: LGBT people still face routine discrimination in all areas of their lives. The Government's annual hate crime report revealed a 32 per cent rise in anti-trans hate crimes in the last year, while those based on sexual orientation jumped by 27 percent. What this new research shows is the devastating impact hate and abuse has on LGBT people's mental health and well being. Victims of anti-LGBT hate crime are at far greater risk of experiencing mental health problems compared to other LGBT people and the wider population (Stonewall, 2019, pp 1,2).

The use of the word 'pride' seems very much to the point as Gilligan explains:

> Lest all of this seem to contradict what I described earlier, that being seen and looked at can be one of the most powerful causes of shame, it is worth noticing that being seen and looked at are also necessary pre-conditions for the fullest augmentation of the feeling of pride. The only difference between the two is whether one's flaws, defects, and shortcomings, or one's achievements and distinctions are being seen... The poor man tends to be ignored and disdained when he would like to be noticed, and exposed or attacked when he would like to have his privacy respected. Both constitute forms of slighting (Gilligan, 2000, p.198).

Unfortunately, our present-day society is showing many parallels with the Victorians'. The recent austerity has brought about resentful feelings towards those who are struggling financially and a climate of blame and shame has deliberately been fostered for those who need benefits. Generally, people in receipt of benefit, even those who are in work but on low wages, have been labelled in certain parts of the media as "scroungers" and a political climate of disdain has ensued which has paved the way for the cutting of many benefits and the demonization of those who need them. This vilification is adding to the emotional burden (of anxiety and stress) people are already carrying in trying to make ends meet:

> Couples raising two children while working full-time on the minimum wage are falling £49 a week short of being able to provide their family with a basic, no-frills lifestyle, research has found. The Child Poverty Action Group (CPAG) called for an increase in the government's "national living wage" to allow families to have an acceptable standard of living. Its Cost of a Child report, published on Monday, showed an 11% weekly shortfall for a couple raising two children at the point they are aged three and seven. Worse, however, was the deficit for lone parents, who every week fall 20% short of being able to provide a level of living for their children defined as acceptable by public opinion (Press Association, 2018, p.1).

What I hope to show is that these stresses and strains will be felt by children too, and to the detriment of their well-being but how has this negative attitude come about?

> Attitudes are informed by knowledge and information, and Delvaux and Rinne (2009) report that there is consistent anecdotal evidence that recipients of awareness raising materials on poverty are surprised by evidence of its prevalence and severity in the UK. This suggests, agreeing with Handley (2009), that the public is not well informed and that opinions may not be well founded in knowledge. Discourses about poverty and its meaning are influenced by many sources including politics, academia and the media. ...The media plays an important role in communicating government policies and forming attitudes (Kendrick et al., 2008). However the issue of poverty per se is rarely discussed in the media, {Yet} even though there are many times more people in poverty than play for Premiership football clubs or quaff £100

> bottles of champagne in exotic nightclubs, there is no comparison with the amount of column inches or airtime devoted to them. And when journalists deal with poverty, too often the result is negative, with little or no attempt to understand or explain what life is like for those on the bottom rung of the economic ladder (Seymour, 2009, p.8).
>
> David Seymour is a well-known and experienced journalist and editor of popular newspapers, and so his opinion is influential testimony to the shortcomings of the media as a source of information about poverty for the public. A research study by McKendrick et al., (2008), based on systematic content analysis of news coverage of poverty also found that poverty is very rarely the direct focus of a news story but is only mentioned in relation to other more newsworthy events such as government policy. They also found that the voices of the poor are rarely reported and that the language of news coverage can also be superficial, dealing in clichés and standard rhetoric (McKendrick et al., 2008). Seymour (2009) goes further and accuses the press of the tendency to stereotype the poor into dramatic but often pejorative roles such as hero, villain or victim, or to stigmatize groups that are poor – single mothers are deemed feckless, recipients of welfare benefits are called scroungers. This resulted in two distinct categories of defining poverty "deserving" and "undeserving" poor (Redden, 2014, p.32–33) (Davies et al, 2014, p.7–8).

What are the origins of this climate of shame? Gilligan offers one theory:

> ...It is worth noting that the rulers of any society, just like the prison guards, have an interest in pursuing the strategies I described earlier: "You scratch my back and I'll scratch yours" and "Divide and conquer". This is accomplished in the macrocosm of society just as it is in the microcosm of the prison, by lulling the

> middle class into accepting its subordination to, and exploitation by, the upper class, by giving the middle class a class subordinate to itself (the lower class) which it can exploit, and to whom it can feel superior, thus distracting the middle class from the resentment it might otherwise feel and express toward the upper class. The subordinate classes (middle and lower) are divided into predator and prey, respectively, and are more likely to fight against each other than against the ruling class, which makes them easier for the ruling class to control. (E.g., middle class voters are angrier at "welfare queens" than they are at members of the Forbes 400 – whom they rather tend to admire, and would like to emulate) (Gilligan, 2000, p.186). {Substitute "welfare scroungers" for "welfare queens".}

This perhaps explains why, during the recent period of austerity, some British newspapers directed their vitriol against benefit "scroungers" as opposed to the powerful global businesses who failed to pay their due taxes? ("UK: Daily Mail and Misleading Articles on Disability Benefits" (The DAA News Network, 2017, p.1) and "Amazon ordered to repay Euros 250m by EU over "illegal tax advantages" (Rankin, 2017, p.1).

The paring back of benefit payments and sanctions are adversely affecting the most vulnerable in society – people with physical/mental disability and those with mental illness and children. People with physical disabilities have been found "fit for work" and died the following week: "More than 2,300 died after 'fit for work' assessment – DWP figures" (BBC, 2015), and people with mental health difficulties have taken their own lives having been told that they are no longer eligible for financial support (Armstrong, 2015, pp.1-11). "Benefit sanctions are "devastating" for claimants and can lead to destitution, crime, suicide, and throw up barriers to employment, a wide-ranging report probing the effects of removing payments from Salford's residents has claimed" (Cowburn, 2016, p.2).

The Joseph Rowntree Foundation has carried out a systematic

> review of international research on the impact of benefit sanctions. This finds, mainly from US research, that sanctions are successful in getting people off benefits, but this may be because they are dropping out of the system altogether, rather than going into decent work. European studies show that the use of sanctions is likely to lead to worse employment outcomes (lower pay and more likely to be back on benefits) than if sanctions are not used. This is because the threat or use of sanctions makes people take lower-quality jobs than if they had been allowed to wait for a better opportunity (The Guardian, 2013, p.3).

People with severe mental illness tend to be living on low incomes and in deprived inner city environments because they experience greater difficulty in securing and retaining jobs and stable housing:

> Faced with increasing financial precarity and uncertainty, households and communities are regularly engaged in the hard work of 'getting by' on low-income social security in an attempt to secure, or at least come close to meeting, their basic needs (Lister, 2004; Patrick, 2014). The coping strategies drawn upon include borrowing money, reducing fuel and food and friends, making use of foodbanks, restricting expenditure to the 'basis {sic} necessities' and not engaging in social or recreational activities (Cooper, 2014; Patrick, 2014; Pemberton et al., 2014; Dermott and Pomati, 2015; Garthwaite et al., 2015; Main and Bradshaw, 2016). Whilst these coping strategies help overcome exigent barriers to meeting human needs, this appears to come at a significant physical and psychological cost to those affected by welfare austerity. Research reveals that many feel that their everyday experiences are damaging to their sense of self-worth, and describe feelings of alienation, degradation, shame, stigma and depression (eg. Chase and Walker, 2013; Baumberg, 2016) (Edmiston, 2016, p.266).

The Victorians also believed, like us (for a while), that wealth would "trickle down" to those 'lower' in society. Unfortunately, we seem not to have learned the lessons of the past: that this is not what happens. Instead, we are creating a more and more unequal society:

> The UK has the 7th most unequal incomes of 30 countries in the developed world, but is about average in terms of wealth inequality. While the top fifth have 40% of the country's income and 60% of the country's wealth, the bottom fifth have only 8% of the income and 1% of the wealth (Equality Trust, 2017).

Inequality has negative impacts on the economy as a whole, property and violent crime levels, and on the health and well-being of individuals in society: "Living in an unequal society causes stress and status anxiety, which may damage your health. In more equal societies people live longer, are less likely to be mentally ill or obese and there are lower rates of infant mortality." (Equality Trust, 2017).

The Joseph Rowntree Foundation has provided a briefing on Universal Credit:

> Stemming the rise in child poverty: More money directly improves children's health and development outcomes, while child poverty scars prospects, costing the Exchequer £6.1bn per year in lost tax revenue and additional benefit spending. From April 2017, all families with children making a new claim will receive £545 per year less financial support. Families will also receive no additional support for a third or subsequent child (with a few exceptions). This policy alone is likely to push an extra 200,000 children into poverty in 2020/21 (Joseph Rowntree Foundation, 2017, p.1).

The Joseph Rowntree Foundation report is quite clear "...child poverty scars prospects, costing the Exchequer £6.1bn per year in lost tax revenue and additional benefit spending". So apart from the monetary factor, how does their claim tie in with theory? Maslow's hierarchy of need is pertinent here:

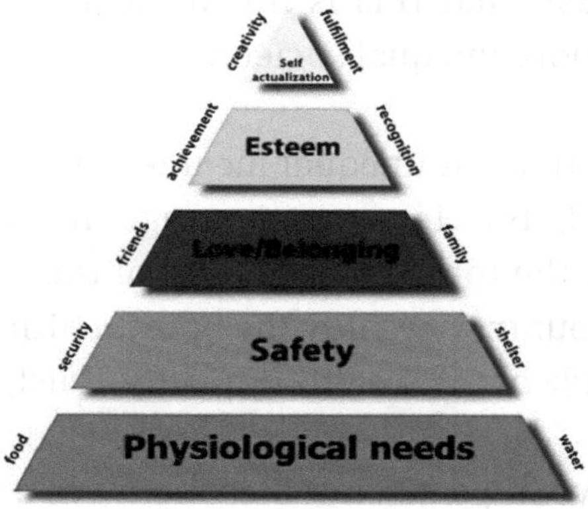

Maslow's theory is that the lower levels of the pyramid of needs must be more or less met before the higher ones can be attained. A child whose physiological needs for food, accommodation, warmth and security are not adequately being met will not be able to go on to form healthy, strong relationships, achieve good self-esteem and fulfil his/her potential (Maslow, 1954,).

> Half of the children needing help from food banks last summer were in primary school and more than a quarter were under the age of five, according to research. The UK's biggest food bank network, the Trussell Trust, has revealed that 67,500 three-day emergency food packages went to children in July and August 2016 – 4,000 more than in the preceding two months. The research shows that 47% of the children receiving supplies from food banks were aged 5–11, while 27% were under five and a fifth were aged 12–16. Samantha Stapley, operations manager for England at the Trussell Trust, said the statistics highlighted "just how close to crisis many families are. She added: "As a nation, we also must address the reasons why families with children are referred to food banks in the first place. "...Imran Hussain, director of policy, rights

> and advocacy at Child Poverty Action Group, described the data as incredibly worrying but not surprising. "Children are twice as likely to be poor than pensioners," he said. "The poverty rate for children is 30% and for pensioners it's 16%. The trajectory for child poverty is that it will hit 5 million by 2022" (Marsh, 2017, pp.1–2).

Joy Ewing states that

> poor children have difficulties regulating emotions leading to mental illness; the stress of poverty can hurt the working memory; less efficient auditory processing abilities; higher risk of high blood pressure and other physical health problems (Ewing, 2016,).

She cites the reasons for these as the

> relationship between nurturing during childhood and the growth of brain tissue. Poor parents were more likely to have poor nurturing skills; poor nutrition; stress taxes the brain, leaving it less bandwidth to solve complex cognitive problems, harming long term decision-making ability; a child's brain is still developing and is especially vulnerable to environmental effects and experiences (Ewing, 2016, pp.1–3).

Ewing cites the following pernicious cycle:

> Child {sic} who are poor are 7 times more likely {to} drop out of school between the age 16–24. A higher percentage of young adults (31%) without a high school diploma live in poverty, compared to the 24% of young people who finished high school. Children that live below the poverty line are 1.3 times more likely to have developmental delays or learning disabilities than those

who don't live in poverty. 40% of poor children are not prepared for primary school (Ewing, 2016, p.1).

Gilligan doesn't mince his words and calls poverty the "deadliest form" of violence:

> In Boston, black babies in the inner city die before their first birthdays at three times the rate of white babies... Medical professionals know how to prevent that high a rate of premature deaths. By applying the principles of preventive medicine to this problem, and treating it as a public health issue, it is possible to document the fact that these premature deaths are not caused primarily by the behaviour of the individual mothers involved, but rather, by structural social and economic factors that are beyond the control of any individual mother.
>
> A recent study conducted by epidemiologists at the Centers of Disease Control, of the U.S. Public Health Service, concluded that only about one-third of the "excess mortality" suffered by blacks (relative to whites) aged thirty-five to fifty-four was associated with any of the known health risks, such as smoking, hypertension, diabetes, obesity, alcohol consumption, and so forth. The remaining two-thirds could only be accounted for by the direct and indirect effects of low socio-economic status itself, i.e., the relative deprivation or poverty that blacks suffer from at vastly higher rates than whites; low family income, unequal access to health care, and the pathogenic (indeed, lethal) stresses caused by lower socioeconomic class position, racial discrimination, social rejection, and unemployment (Gilligan, 2000, p.193).

Ground-breaking neuro-scientific research in America at Dr Kimberly Noble's laboratory at Columbia University in New York, is showing that family income has a big impact on the brains of children:

> {Noble} is among the handful of neuroscientists and paediatricians who've seen increasing evidence that poverty itself – and not factors like nutrition, language exposure, family stability, or prenatal issues, as previously thought – may diminish the growth of a child's brain. Dr Noble, in collaboration with neuroscientist Martha Farah, has been investigating the observation that poor kids tended to perform worse academically than their better-off peers. They wanted to investigate the neurocognitive underpinnings of this relationship – to trace the long-standing correlation between socioeconomic status and academic performance back to specific parts of the brain...Farah, Noble and other scientists ... began using magnetic resonance imaging (MRI) scans to examine the brains of children across the socioeconomic spectrum. The results were striking. In one study, Farah looked at 283 MRIs and found that kids from poorer, less-educated families tended to have thinner subregions of the prefrontal cortex – a part of the brain strongly associated with executive functioning – than better-off kids. That could explain weaker academic achievement and even lower IQs. In 2015, Noble co-authored the largest study to date. Using MRI, researchers examined 1,099 children and young adults, and found the brains of those with higher family income and more parental education had larger surface areas than their poorer, less-educated peers. The strongest correlation came in brain regions associated with language and executive functioning. What's more, the data indicated that small increases in family income had a much larger impact on the brains of the poorest children than similar increases among wealthier children (Mariani, 2017, pp.2–3).

Perhaps the most conclusive evidence of the detrimental effects of poverty on children's mental health (and the problems we may be creating for individuals and society for the future by making families poorer) is to be found in "Poor Mental Health – the links between child poverty and mental health problems" a report by the Children's Society (March 2016) by David Ayre.

> The End Child Poverty coalition outlines in its Unhealthy Lives report that children in families in poverty are over three times more likely to suffer from mental health problems than their more affluent peers. For children in poverty, 1 in 40 children aged 5–10 engages in self-harm, compared to fewer than 1 in 100 of those with high socio-economic status. Likewise, a review of poverty and mental health by the Centre for Social Justice highlights that children and adults from the lowest 20% of household income are three times more likely to have common mental health problems than those in the richest 20%, and nine times as likely to have psychotic disorders...
>
> The recent report by the Children's Commissioners for the UK – which looks at welfare reform and austerity measures – outlined their deep apprehension over future austerity measures, given the effect that the benefit cap, the spare room subsidy, benefit sanctions and other measures have had on the household income for families already living on low incomes (Ayre, 2016, p.13).

Debt is mentioned in Edith's notes as being a cause for particular distress: ("they got into debt and this greatly upset her"). The Money Advice Service, set up by government (https://www.moneyadviceservice.org.uk), estimates that 8.2 million adults (16.1% of the population) are experiencing problem debt.

> The Children's Society's research has shown that living in a family that has experienced problem debt has a real impact on children – both in terms of the emotional impact and in terms of the ways in which they seek to protect their parents as far as they can... with around half of parents surveyed (47%) saying that their financial

> situation caused their children emotional distress, and a quarter saying that it resulted in their children feeling stressed or anxious... This is further reinforced by evidence from the Royal College of Psychiatrists that sets out how 'debt may have indirect effects on household psychological well-being over time, as it impacts on feelings of economic pressure, parental depression, conflict-based family relationships, and potential mental health problems among children (Ayre, 2016, p.15).

Tying in with Maslow's basic needs, housing is a major issue for poor families:

> Research by the Chartered Institute of Environmental Health has demonstrated that there is a significant relationship between poor housing and mental health problems in children. The evidence that they present suggests that there is a causal link between some physical conditions, such as dampness and overcrowding, 'both on a physiological and psychological basis... Research by Moat has shown that the £26,000 benefit cap currently in place means that two bedroom houses will be beyond the reach of families in receipt of Housing Benefit in most local authorities within eight years, and that within 10 years most one bedroom houses would become unaffordable. This is a situation which will be further exacerbated by the additional reduction to the Cap set out in the Welfare Reform and Work Bill, which will see it reduced to £23,000 in London and £20,000 outside London, alongside a four year freeze to Local Housing Allowance rates... This suggests that there could be longer term implications for the development of mental health problems in children and young people in poverty if Government policy is contributing to a situation where families find it harder to secure appropriate and stable housing (Ayre, 2016, p.17).

"Fuel poverty" is also becoming a serious issue for poor families.

> There are serious physical health consequences as a result of growing up in a cold home, as evidenced by the Marmot Review in 2011. This research outlines how more than 1 in 4 adolescents living in cold housing 'are at risk of multiple mental health problems' compared to 1 in 20 adolescents who have always lived in warm housing. Research by Sheffield Hallam University has shown that growing up in a cold home is linked to an increased risk of depression and anxiety (Ayre, 2016, p.18).

The Children's Society report goes on to express their deep concern that although

> the Conservative election manifesto and the Department for Education have made commitments regarding increased funding for mental health services and improved waiting times, there is no indication that children in poverty will be recognised as an at-risk group (Ayre, 2016, p.19).

Moreover,

> ...analysis of our FOI of Mental Health Trusts showed that more often than not CAMHS [Child and Adolescent Mental Health Services] service providers did not ask specific questions in the referral forms and assessments about the standard of housing that children and young people lived in. This suggests that there is insufficient recognition of the evidence outlined above and its implications (Ayre, 2016, p.18).

> "Jacob Rees-Mogg thinks food banks are 'uplifting'. For me, they're a necessity." (Bly, 2017, pp.1–3).

Chapter 4

ELIZABETH

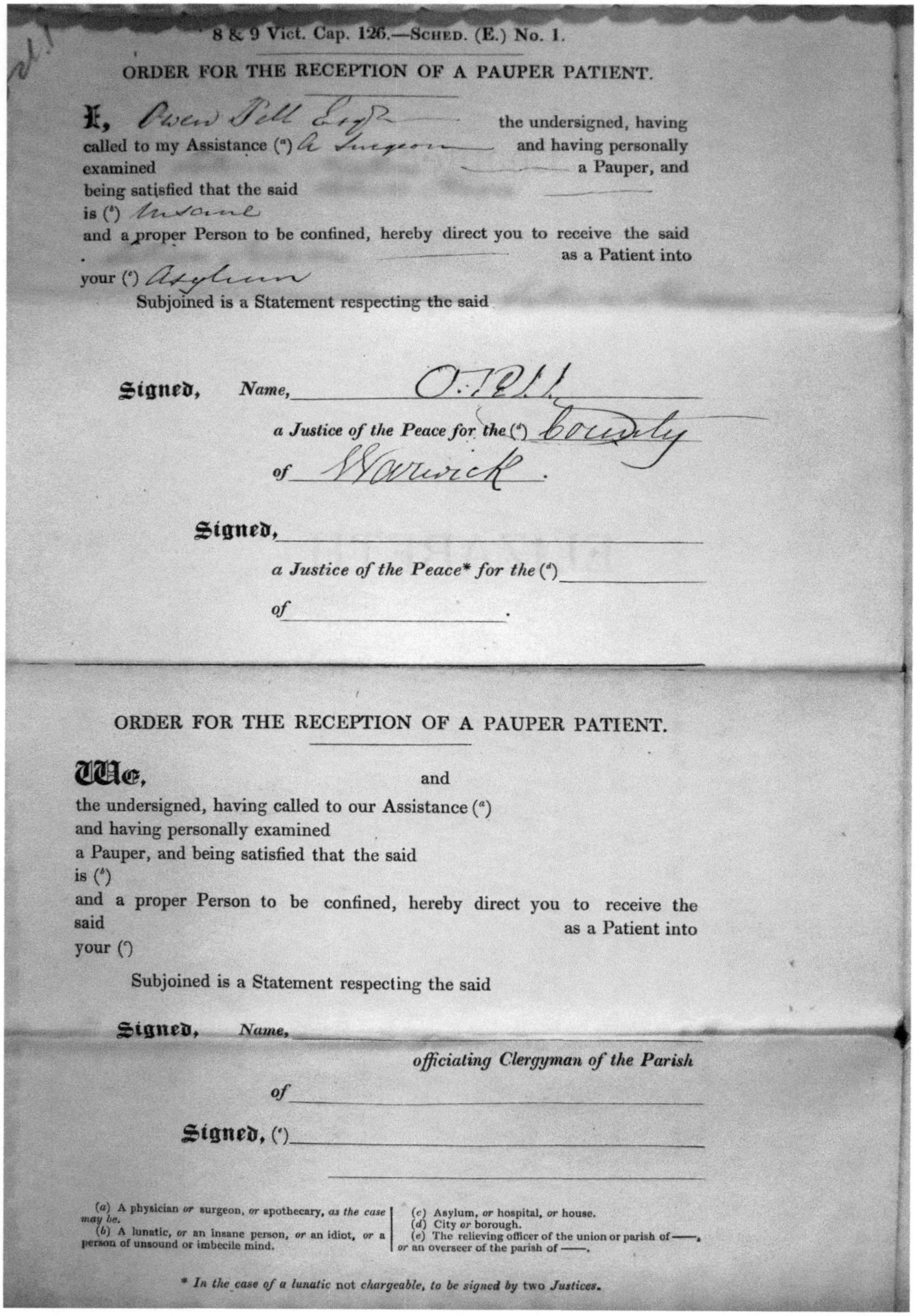

8 & 9 Vict. Cap. 126.—Sched. (E.) No. 1.

ORDER FOR THE RECEPTION OF A PAUPER PATIENT.

I, Owen Pell Esqr the undersigned, having called to my Assistance (a) a Surgeon and having personally examined a Pauper, and being satisfied that the said is (b) Insane and a proper Person to be confined, hereby direct you to receive the said as a Patient into your (c) Asylum

Subjoined is a Statement respecting the said

Signed, *Name,* O. Pell

a Justice of the Peace for the (d) County

of Warwick.

Signed,

a Justice of the Peace for the* (d)

of .

ORDER FOR THE RECEPTION OF A PAUPER PATIENT.

We, and

the undersigned, having called to our Assistance (a)

and having personally examined

a Pauper, and being satisfied that the said

is (b)

and a proper Person to be confined, hereby direct you to receive the said as a Patient into

your (c)

Subjoined is a Statement respecting the said

Signed, *Name,*

officiating Clergyman of the Parish

of

Signed, (e)

(a) A physician *or* surgeon, *or* apothecary, *as the case may be.*
(b) A lunatic, *or* an insane person, *or* an idiot, *or* a person of unsound or imbecile mind.
(c) Asylum, *or* hospital, *or* house.
(d) City *or* borough.
(e) The relieving officer of the union or parish of ——, *or* an overseer of the parish of ——.

* *In the case of a lunatic* not *chargeable, to be signed by* two *Justices.*

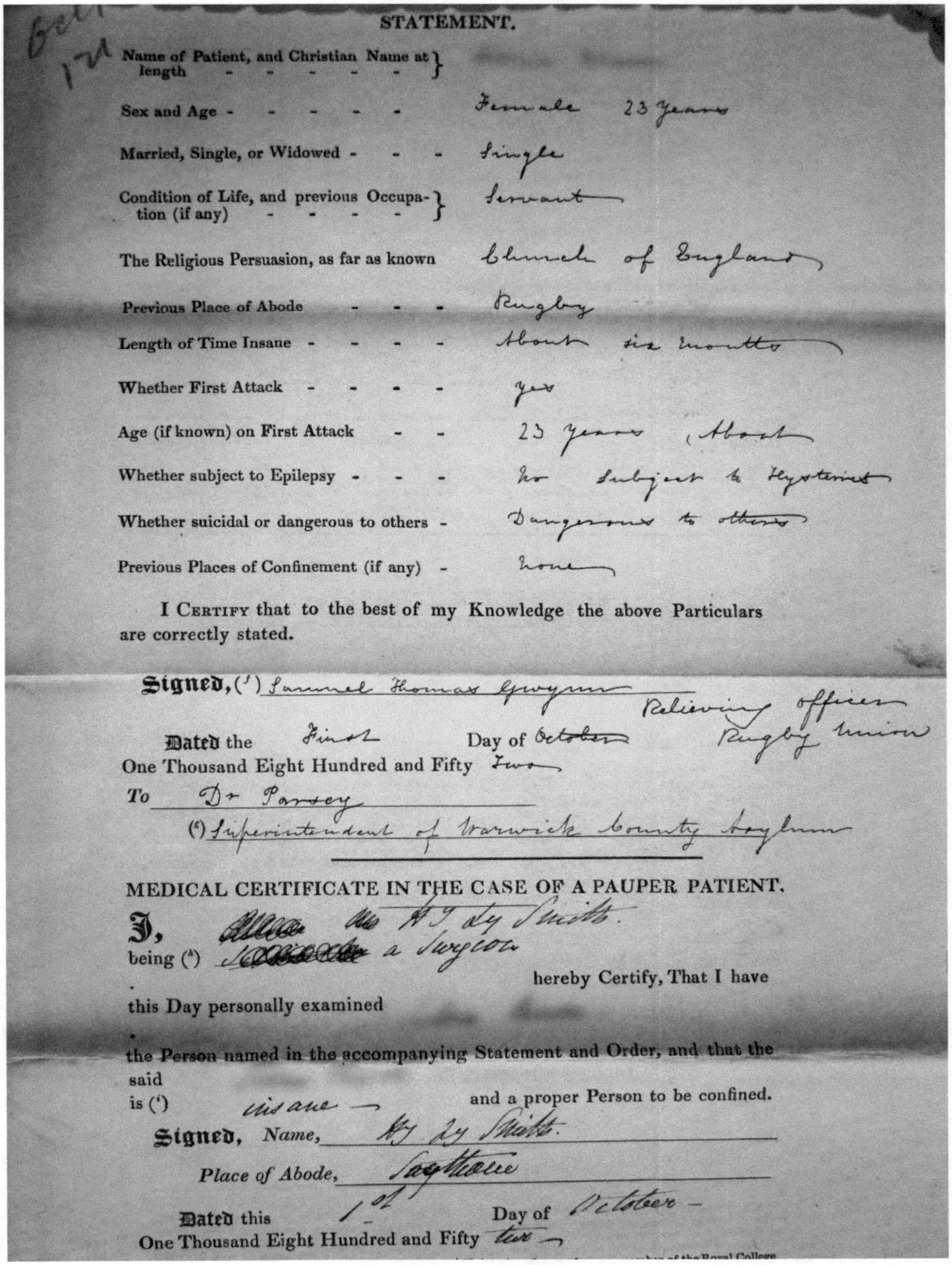

STATEMENT.

Name of Patient, and Christian Name at length	[illegible]
Sex and Age	Female 23 Years
Married, Single, or Widowed	Single
Condition of Life, and previous Occupation (if any)	Servant
The Religious Persuasion, as far as known	Church of England
Previous Place of Abode	Rugby
Length of Time Insane	About six months
Whether First Attack	Yes
Age (if known) on First Attack	23 years (About
Whether subject to Epilepsy	No Subject to Hysterics
Whether suicidal or dangerous to others	Dangerous to others
Previous Places of Confinement (if any)	None

I CERTIFY that to the best of my Knowledge the above Particulars are correctly stated.

Signed, (1) Samuel Thomas Gwynn Relieving officer Rugby Union

Dated the First Day of October One Thousand Eight Hundred and Fifty Two

To Dr Parsey

(5) Superintendent of Warwick County Asylum

MEDICAL CERTIFICATE IN THE CASE OF A PAUPER PATIENT.

I, [illegible] H T dy Smith. being (a) [illegible] a Surgeon hereby Certify, That I have this Day personally examined the Person named in the accompanying Statement and Order, and that the said is (c) insane and a proper Person to be confined.

Signed, Name, H T dy Smith.

Place of Abode, Southam

Dated this 1st Day of October –

One Thousand Eight Hundred and Fifty two

Opposite and above: Ref: CR1664/250

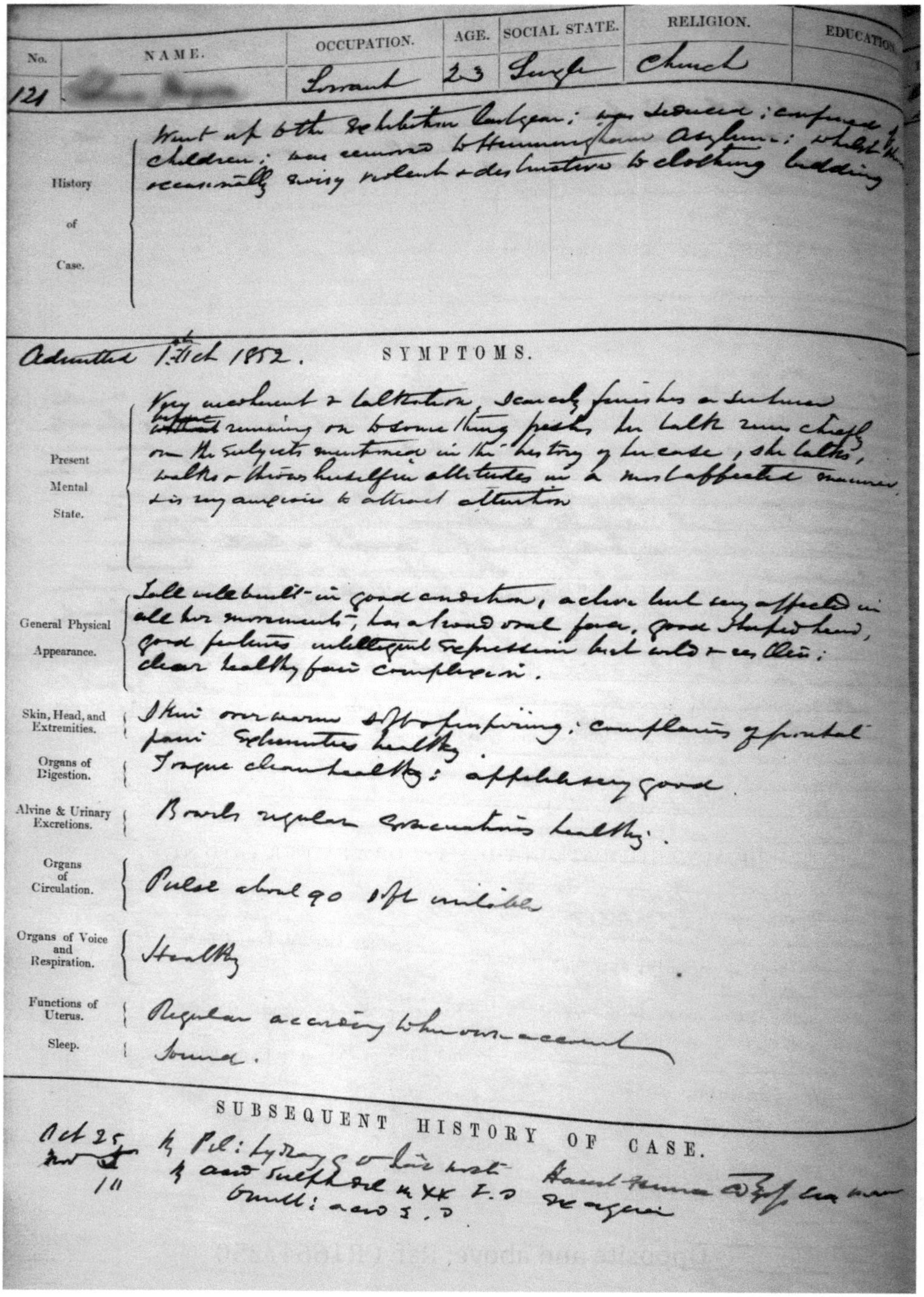
No.	NAME.	OCCUPATION.	AGE.	SOCIAL STATE.	RELIGION.	EDUCATION
121	[illegible]	Servant	23	Single	Church	

History of Case. — Went up to the Exhibition last year; was seduced; confined of children; was removed to Hammersmith Asylum; whilst there occasionally noisy violent & destructive to clothing bedding

Admitted 1st Oct 1852. SYMPTOMS.

Present Mental State. — Very incoherent & inattention, scarcely finishes a sentence before running on to something fresh, her talk runs chiefly on the subjects mentioned in the history of her case, she talks, walks & throws herself in attitudes in a most affected manner & is very anxious to attract attention

General Physical Appearance. — Tall well built in good condition, active but very affected in all her movements; has a broad oval face, good shaped head, good features intelligent expression but wild & restless: clear healthy fair complexion.

Skin, Head, and Extremities. — Skin over warm & soft & perspiring: complains of frontal pain. Extremities healthy.

Organs of Digestion. — Tongue clean healthy: appetite very good.

Alvine & Urinary Excretions. — Bowels regular, excretions healthy.

Organs of Circulation. — Pulse about 90 soft unirritable

Organs of Voice and Respiration. — Healthy

Functions of Uterus. — Regular according to her own account

Sleep. — Sound.

SUBSEQUENT HISTORY OF CASE.

Oct 25 ℞ Pil: [illegible]
Nov [illegible] 11 [illegible]

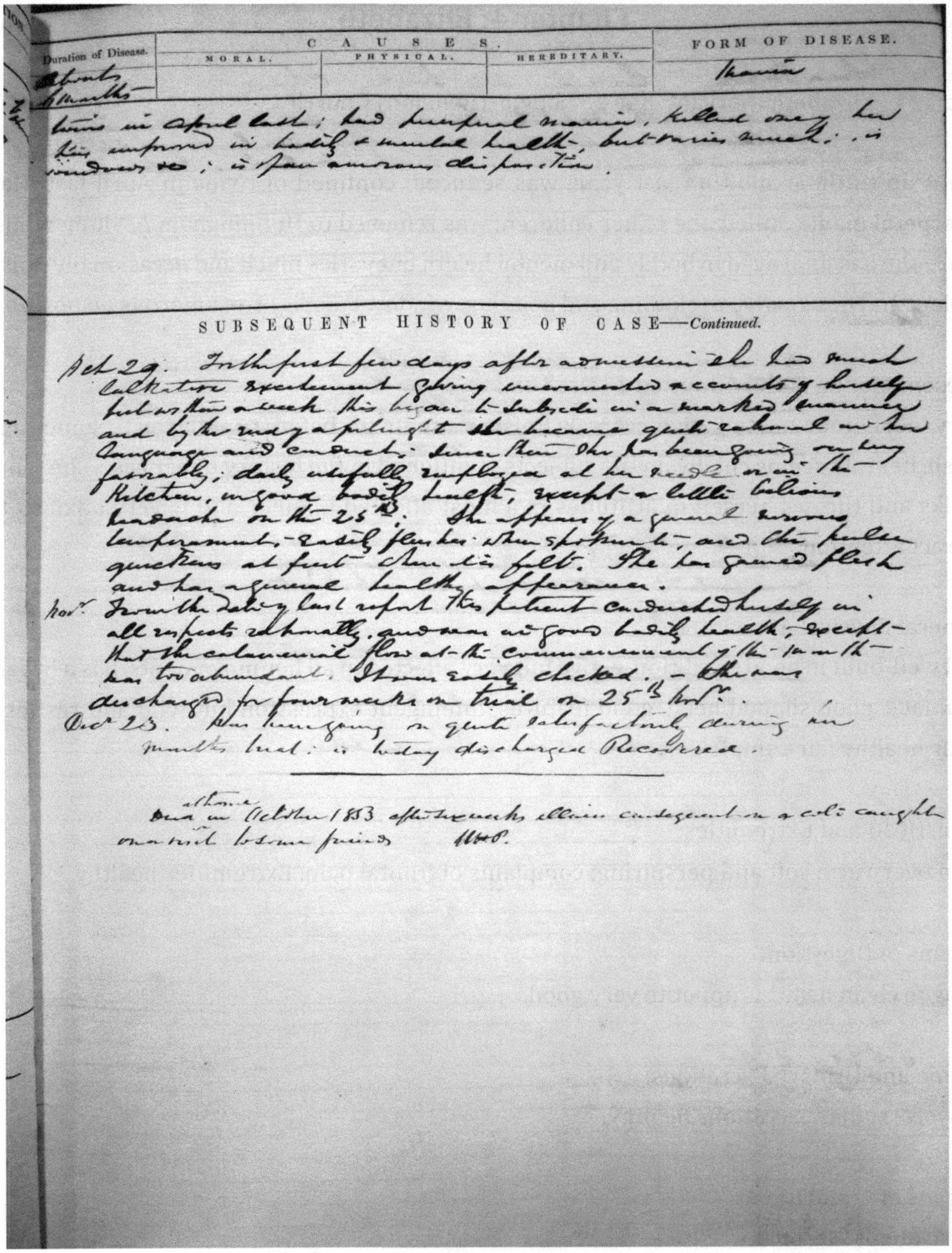

Duration of Disease.	CAUSES. MORAL.	PHYSICAL.	HEREDITARY.	FORM OF DISEASE.
About 6 months				Mania

twins in April last; had puerperal mania, killed one of her ... improved in bodily & mental health, but varies much: is ... windows &c; is of an amorous disposition.

SUBSEQUENT HISTORY OF CASE—*Continued.*

Oct 29. For the first few days after admission she had much talkative excitement giving unconnected accounts of herself but in less than a week this began to subside in a marked manner and by the end of a fortnight she became quite rational in her language and conduct. Since then she has been going on very favorably; daily usefully employed at her needle or in the kitchen, in good bodily health, except a little bilious headache on the 25th. She appears of a general nervous temperament, easily flushes when spoken to, and the pulse quickens at first when it is felt. She has gained flesh and has a general healthy appearance.

Novr. From the date of last report this patient conducted herself in all respects rationally, and was in good bodily health, except that the catamenial flow at the commencement of the month was too abundant. It was easily checked. – She was discharged for four weeks on trial on 25th Novr.

Decr 23. Has been going on quite satisfactorily during her month's trial: is today discharged Recovered.

Died at home in October 1883 after six weeks illness consequent on a cold caught on a visit to some friends   W.H.P.

Opposite and above: Ref: CR 1664/617

Chapter 4: Elizabeth

"No 121 Elizabeth. Servant Age 23 Single (Religion) Church

Went up to the exhibition last year; was seduced; confined of twins in April last. Had puerperal mania. Killed one of her children; was removed to Hunningham Asylum; whilst there she has improved in bodily and mental health but varies much and occasionally noisy, violent and destructive to clothing and bedding, windows too; is of an amorous disposition.

Present Mental State: Admitted 1st Oct 1852
Very incoherent and talkative, scarcely finishes a sentence before running on to something fresh, her talk seems chiefly on the subjects mentioned in the history of her case, she talks, walks and throws herself in attitudes in a most affected manner and is very anxious to attract attention.

General Physical Appearance:
Tall well-built in good condition, active but very affected in all her movements, has a broad, oval face, good shaped head, good features, intelligent expression but wild and restless; clear healthy fair complexion.

Skin, Head and Extremities:
Skin overwarm soft and perspiring; complains of frontal pain. Extremities healthy.

Organs of Digestion:
Tongue clean healthy; appetite very good.

Alvine and Urinary Excretions:
Bowels regular excretions healthy.

Organs of Circulation:
Pulse about 90 soft ?

Organs of Voice and Respiration:

Healthy

Functions of Uterus:
Regular according to her own account.

Sleep:
Sound

Subsequent History of Case – continued.

Oct 29 In the first few days after admission she had much talkative excitement giving unwarranted accounts of herself but within a week this began to subside in a marked manner and by the end of a fortnight she became quite natural in her language and conduct; since then she has been going on very favourably; daily usefully employed at her needle or in the kitchen, in good bodily health, except a little bilious headache on the 25th. She appears of a general nervous temperament, easily flushes when spoken to, and the pulse quickens at first when it is felt. She has gained flesh and a general healthy appearance.

Nov Since the date of last report this patient conducted herself in all respects normally, and was in good bodily health, except that the catameinial flow at the commencement of the month was too abundant. It was easily checked. She was discharged for four weeks on trial on 25th Nov.
Dec 23 Has been going on quite satisfactorily during her month's trial. Is today discharged. Recovered.

Died at home in October 1853 after two weeks' illness consequent on a cold caught on a visit to some friends."

Elizabeth's life story is a tragic one. The Census confirms what we read in the medical notes: 23 Apr 1852 – M baptised at Saint Andrew, Rugby. Mother – Elizabeth. 25 Apr 1852 – N baptised at Saint Andrew, Rugby. Mother – Elizabeth. 3rd May 1852 – M buried, aged 10 days, at Saint Andrew, Rugby. 14th May 1852 – N buried, aged 26 days, at Saint Andrew, Rugby. 6th August 1853 – Elizabeth buried, aged 24 years, at Saint Andrew, Rugby. We may assume that Elizabeth was admitted to Hunningham Asylum sometime before 3rd May (the day that M was buried). The twins must have been born on or around the 18th April. N died at just under a month old. It's quite possible that she died due to a lack of milk.

Elizabeth was a servant, so how and why did she go to the Great Exhibition of 1851?

> Queen Victoria opened the Exhibition on 1 May, on schedule. She became a frequent visitor. At first the price of admission was £3 for gentlemen, £2 for ladies. They came in throngs, in their elegant carriages, leaving them at a separate entrance to be valet-parked. Saturday mornings were reserved for invalids. From 24th May the masses were let in for only a shilling a head. And they came in their thousands, factory workers sent by their employers, country villagers sent by benevolent landowners, strings of schoolchildren. The country men came wearing their best smocks, staring at all the Londoners and foreigners. The travel agent Thomas Cook arranged special excursion trains. A third-class return ticket from York cost only five shillings. One old lady even walked, all the way from Penzance. There was even a mysterious Chinese man in full mandarin robes, who stepped forward as the royal procession passed. He was treated, just in case he was important, as a visiting dignitary, but he turned out to be the captain of a Chinese junk moored in the river.
>
> By the time the Exhibition closed, on 11 October, over six million people had gone through the turnstiles. Instead of the loss initially

> predicted, the Exhibition made a profit of £186,000, most of which was used to create the South Kensington museums. Those were Albert's memorial. His Queen commissioned the statue of him, sitting under a gilt canopy opposite the Royal Albert Hall with a copy of the Exhibition catalogue on his knee (Picard, 2009).

Postpartum psychosis (puerperal mania) is a severe mental illness and is usually treated as an emergency. Women can experience a variety of symptoms and often lose contact with reality, making it very difficult for them to meet their baby's needs and their own. The Royal College of Psychiatrists publish a useful guide, (rcpsych, 2019).

Elizabeth was a product of the wider Victorian 'macrosystem' and the sub-culture of her family. Urie Bronfenbrenner may be pertinent here. He uses as a source Vygotsky's theory , the "sociohistorical evolution of the mind" in his Ecological Systems Theory of the developing person...

> that from earliest childhood onward the development of one's characteristics as a person depends in significant degree on the options that are available in a given culture at a given point in its history (Bronfenbrenner, 1992, p.228).

Most Victorian women lived their lives wearing a metaphorical straitjacket. They were expected to carry most of the responsibility for the sexual mores of the time, but in other aspects of their lives, they were powerless. In many ways society placed a double bind onto girls and women. Not only were they the subjects of sexual scapegoating, at whom the whole of society pointed the accusatory finger if they "transgressed", but many girls were kept in ignorance of sexual matters and their own reproductory systems due to embarrassment and prudery. Women were infantilised. What made it even more difficult for women was the stigma associated with the "fallen woman":

> What was essential to Victorian England was that women stayed "pure" (there was unsurprisingly, no parallel narrative of a "fallen

> man") and what happened to the mothers who arrived with their babies at the Foundling hospital, as played out across the art and literature and music of the century, was to be a lesson to all the rest. The "fault" was all female, and for the women who fell, the drop was very far indeed (Moorhead, 2015, pp.3–4).

Times and attitudes change, but it is clear that any woman who had sex outside marriage, for whatever reason, in Victorian times was deemed a "prostitute".

> Any discussion of prostitution in the 19th century must begin by saying we have no idea of the numbers involved. In 1791, a police magistrate estimated (and he used the words 'estimate' and 'conjecture') that there were 50,000 prostitutes in London. Yet the word 'prostitute' was not used entirely the way we would use it today, i.e. to refer only to women {sic} sold their bodies for sex. In the 19th century, many people used it more widely, to refer to women who were living with men outside marriage, or women who had had illegitimate children, or women who perhaps had relations with men, but for pleasure rather than money. (Flanders, 2014, p.1).

Elizabeth's pregnancy would have been very difficult to hide, and she would have experienced universal condemnation and disdain and consequently felt the most acute shame. In some of the workhouses women who had had illegitimate children

> were made to wear a yellow top (which earned them the name 'jacket women') instead of the blue one worn by other paupers. This practice was forbidden in 1844, although some unions, such as the one at Gressenhall, continued to issue the jackets for at least another 20 years (Fowler, 2014, p.77).

The incarceration of unmarried pregnant women in the workhouses and asylums was common.

> Indeed, the complex picture of society in Pat Thane and Tanya Evans' new history of single motherdom, Sinners? Scroungers? Saints? Unmarried Motherhood in 20th Century England (Oxford University Press), shows that unmarried co-habitation, for example, was common as far back as the 1800s, when records first began. Thane, ... argues that there has never been such a thing as the ideal British family unit, but instead a whole raft of diverse arrangements to which the authorities turned a blind eye – until they had to pay for it. Only the most visible, vulnerable cases – the unsupported women – were ruthlessly singled out for scapegoating, since they had been seen as a drain on the parish purse ever since the first Poor Law in 1576. And when the earliest form of social insurance finally came into effect in 1925, it was granted to widowed mothers but not divorced or unmarried ones – a malicious piece of legislation clearly intended to deter women with unconventional lives from living off the state (Paton, 2012, p.3).

Most unmarried mothers were obliged to give up their babies for adoption, (or hope that they would be accepted by the Foundling hospital, for example) as they had no means to support themselves and were the objects of public humiliation and condemnation. As nothing comes out of a vacuum, compare the vilification single mothers still receive from the tabloid press today.

Added to this oppression was the overwhelming paternalism of the mental health system at the time: male doctors, having male views and patrician attitudes to female suffering, and female asylum attendants adopting those attitudes because of societal indoctrination and their lowlier position. Indeed, Elizabeth is suffering from "triple jeopardy": she is female; she is a pauper and she is mentally ill. As an example of the female jeopardy "it is agreed by all alienist physicians" wrote one doctor, "that girls are far more likely to inherit insanity from their mothers than from the other parent" (Showalter, 2004, p.67). The male doctors believed that the functions of the uterus were major risk factors for women's mental ill-health, and therefore the onset of menarche at adolescence, menstruation, childbearing and the menopause were all thought to be potential triggers. Dr Parsey notes treatment of Elizabeth's "catameinial" (menstrual) flow for this reason. (These attitudes were taken to an extreme when a form of female genital mutilation (FGM) (clitoridectomy and removal of the labia) was performed on women a few years later as a cure for female insanity by Dr Isaac Baker Brown a member of the Obstetrical Society of London.) FGM remains very much in the spotlight today, but the fight against this particular form of abuse against women has really only just begun.

Under the heading "Does Society cause excessive female mental illness?" Rogers and Pilgrim look at 'vulnerability factors' and 'provoking agents':

> Women whose personalities were characterised by low self-esteem were more likely to experience the onset of depression than those who had high self-esteem. The work of Brown and Harris in the 1970s has been extended in the interim... Drawing upon the work of Gilbert (1992) and Unger (1984), they elaborate their position about depression and the experience of life events. They conclude that the probability of depression increases not necessarily with loss or threatened loss *per se* but with the coexistence of humiliation and/or entrapment. Gilbert and Unger note that depression is commonly associated with feeling defeated, humiliated and entrapped (Rogers and Pilgrim, 2014, pp.39–40).

The findings of this research give pause for thought with regard to "female passivity", a quality expected of Victorian women in general.

Jerry Tew makes a convincing case for a social approach to mental health care. He transposes the biomedical model language (for example:

'mental illness', 'symptoms', 'diagnosis', 'treatment', 'cure', 'care') for social model language (mental distress, experience, meaning, action planning, empowerment, self-directed support) respectively. He states that:

> It is important to start with the assumption that all expressions of mental distress are ways in which we may be trying to express 'the meaning of our lives' (Plumb, 1999, p 471). So, instead of writing them off as 'symptoms' of 'mental illness', distress experiences should be respected and taken seriously as an attempt to communicate something – perhaps about an injustice or a 'problem of living' – which may be very hard to express by more conventional means (Tew, 2011, p.16).

Tew suggests that:

> Rather than seeking to understand mental distress as a medical *dis-ease*, it may be more helpful to see it as arising out of a state of *un-ease* both with ourselves and our wider social situation. In many situations, we may be able to resolve our unease for ourselves – perhaps through making changes in our lives or through dealing with unresolved issues that are troubling us. In other instances, we may (just about) be able to hold our unease while putting on a 'normal' face to the wider world, however, at some point, this unease may start to come back to the surface, particularly if current life circumstances may be stressful or difficult. If we cannot contain or deal with our unease, this may escalate to the point where it becomes mental distress (Tew, 2011, p.29).

He goes on to explain that

> Although, subjectively, experiences can seem very different, what is perhaps the defining characteristic of all forms of mental distress

> is the disruption of our *personal agency*: our ability to organise ourselves sufficiently in order to deal either with our underlying unease or the ordinary expectations of our social and family lives (Tew, 2011, p.29).

Added to the sexual discrimination she is experiencing is Elizabeth's definition as a pauper. Henry Mayhew wrote a series of articles on the London poor between 1849 and 1852 for two different newspapers, and describes the appalling conditions he found one group of women living in following the birth of a child who subsequently died.

> On a mattress, on the floor, lay a pale-faced girl – 'eighteen years old last twelfth-cake day' – her drawn-up form showing in the patch-work counterpane that covered her. She had just been confined, and the child had died! A little straw, stuffed into an old tick, was all she had to lie upon, and even that had been given up to her by the mother until she was well enough to work again.... The parish, the old woman told me, allowed her 1 s. a week and two loaves. But the doctor ordered her girl to take sago and milk and she was many a time sorely puzzled to get it. The neighbours helped her a good deal, and often sent her part of their unsold greens; – even if it was only the outer leaves of the cabbages, she was thankful for them... 'As long as they kept out of the "big house" (the workhouse) she would not complain (Mayhew, 2012, pp.37–39).

> Poverty was, after all, one of the moral causes of insanity. Women were the majority of recipients of poor-law relief, and poor people were more likely to be committed to institutions than people from the middle or upper classes (Showalter, 2004, p.54).

Victorian doctors seem to have had different ideas as to the causes of insanity. Some thought madness was deviance from socially accepted mores;

some thought it was due to “moral causes” such as stresses and strong emotions which reduced the system’s ability to cope; some thought mental illness had purely physical causes such as infections or imbalances within the physical body; and some thought it was a combination of the above.

> In practice, moral and physical causes were often hard to distinguish. Out of 411 men admitted to Colney Hatch in its first six months, for example, “physical causes” were identified for 140, including intemperance, masturbation, head injury, epilepsy and fever. "Moral" causes were indicated for 89 cases; these included domestic grief, unemployment, loss of property, jealousy, and “over-excitement at the Great Exhibition” (Showalter, 2004, p.30).

It’s worthwhile looking at the photographs of the Statement and Order for Reception of a Pauper Patient proformas (printed at the beginning of the chapter) and the headings signposting the required information in Elizabeth’s case. They very much focus on the physical. It’s clear too, that patients were not really thought of as individuals, with individual needs. There’s no requirement for Elizabeth’s address, her date of birth, her next of kin. It’s hardly surprising that we don’t hear her voice anywhere.

Perhaps it is worth raising here Dr Parsey’s comment in Elizabeth’s notes about her “amorous disposition”. She may have been amorous, she may not. Dr Parsey seems to have believed her behaviour to be inappropriate. He describes her as “tall well-built in good condition ... good shaped head, good features, intelligent expression but wild and restless; clear healthy fair complexion.” The detailed description he gives of Elizabeth could relate to the theory of phrenology, where distinct characteristics of the head and face were believed to denote personality and the propensity to aggressiveness etc. Is he more voluble on her physical appearance than with other patients? It is impossible to know. What is more, we are only able to “see” her though Dr Parsey’s eyes, and his perceptions are very much influenced by the culture in which they both lived. (Indeed, this makes the interpretation of historical documents difficult, because we, too, are influenced by our own culture.)

> Cases of puerperal insanity seemed to violate all of Victorian culture's most deeply cherished ideals of feminine propriety and maternal love. Women with puerperal mania were indifferent to the usual conventions of politeness and decorum in speech, dress, and behaviour; their deviance covered a wide spectrum from eccentricity to infanticide... Whereas maternity was viewed by the Victorians as a pure and almost sacred state, violent puerperal maniacs flaunted their sexuality in ways that shocked physicians... It was during the nineteenth century that the infanticidal woman first became the subject of psychiatric as well as legal discourse. Her crime was the worst that could be imagined by a society that exalted maternity; medical theory struggled to account for it in a way that maintained the mythology of motherhood and maternal instinct... As we would expect, child murder was much more likely to occur in conjunction with illegitimacy, poverty and brutality. These factors, whether or not they were considered by medical specialists, were certainly taken into account by Victorian judges and juries, who were reluctant to sentence infanticidal women to death, and who responded compassionately to the insanity defense generally used in their behalf (Showalter, 2004, pp.58-59).

Unfortunately, the sacred status accorded to maternity in the Victorian mind seems only to have been extended to married women, and also does not seem to apply to 'paupers'.

It is interesting to note, moreover, that Dr Parsey appears to simply discharge Elizabeth. Where did she go? She had no follow-up, and no professional support after discharge. Dr Parsey states that Elizabeth died at home. Thankfully it appears that she was not abandoned by her family and didn't end up in the workhouse. If N had survived and if Elizabeth's family had been unable or unwilling to support them, Elizabeth and N would have been obliged to enter the workhouse because outdoor relief was not given to mothers with illegitimate children. In the workhouse, children were allowed to stay with their mothers until they reached the age of two, then they were separated and "infant mortality was more than 90%" (Moorhead, 2015, p.2).

Mental illness has strong links to the cultural pressures and norms evident in contemporary society. Discrimination and racism, for example, are clear contributory factors for mental illness within black, Asian and minority ethnic (BAME) groups. "For madness, as Soshana Felman has noted, is "quite the opposite of rebellion. Madness is the impasse confronting those whom cultural conditioning has deprived of the very means of protest or self-affirmation." (Showalter, 2004, p.5). There is no doubt that women in Victorian society were very much discriminated against and disempowered. As women they were not allowed a voice, hence writers such as Charlotte, Emily and Anne Bronte publishing their work under pseudonyms, along with George Eliot. "Cultural conditioning" is a phrase which carries a great deal of complexity. There are many cultures and subcultures, after all: national culture, ethnic culture, community culture, family culture. What is more they can all be complex. Family culture (like the other sub-cultures (Bronfenbrenner, 1992, p.229)) can, and often does, include dysfunction, abuse, learned parenting style, religious factors, income - all of which may affect members' mental health; and these patterns are passed down the generations often with the production of a vicious cycle. We have drawn attention to the adverse effects on mental health of childhood sexual abuse, but

> sexual victimization may be part of a wider picture of family disturbance, which could be pathogenic. As Briere and Runtz (1987:371) point out: 'Although symptomatology in adulthood may co-vary with early sexual abuse, in the absence of further data it is not clear whether the former is caused by the latter or whether both are actually a function of some third variable, such as dysfunctional family dynamics.' The risk of childhood sexual abuse seems to be enhanced by a number of factors, such as troubled

> inter-generational attachment relationships in families. These include problems in maternal adult functioning, a negative relationship between the grandmother and mother, and a disrupted pattern of care-giving during the mother's childhood (Leifer *et al.* 2004) (Rogers and Pilgrim, 2014, p.75).

We don't hear Elizabeth's voice, but her behaviour is described. Dr Parsey notes that while at Hunningham, she was "noisy, violent and destructive to clothing and bedding, windows too". (Interestingly, Victorian female psychiatric patients were often destructive of clothing, and Victorian clothing was extremely restrictive.) All behaviour is an attempt at communication, and Elizabeth's behaviour speaks of rage, but anger is usually a secondary emotion. People feel anger because they have been hurt or see something as unjust. Elizabeth's anger and hostile emotions ended in tragedy when she murdered M.

> The first lesson that tragedy teaches (and that morality plays miss) is that *all violence is an attempt to achieve justice,* or what the violent person perceives as justice, for himself or for whomever it is on whose behalf he is being violent, so as to receive whatever retribution or compensation the violent person feels is "due" him or they are "entitled" to or have a "right" to; or so as to prevent those whom one loves or identifies with from being subjected to injustice. Thus, *the attempt to achieve and maintain justice, or to undo or prevent injustice, is the one and only universal cause of violence."* [Author's italics] (Gilligan, 2000, pp.11-12).

James Gilligan is a psychiatrist who has spent his professional life working with violent offenders in America, and he states:

> I have yet to see a serious act of violence that was not provoked by the experience of feeling shamed and humiliated, disrespected and ridiculed, and that did not represent the attempt to prevent or

> undo this "loss of face" – no matter how severe the punishment, even if it includes death.... Perhaps the lesson of all this for society is that when men feel sufficiently impotent and humiliated, the usual assumptions one makes about human behaviour and motivation, such as the wish to eat when starving, the wish to live or stay out of prison at all costs, no longer hold. Einstein taught us that Newton's laws do not hold when objects approach the speed of light; what I have learned about humans is that the "instinct of (physiological) self-preservation" does not hold when one approaches the point of being so overwhelmed by shame that one can only preserve one's self (as a psychological entity) by sacrificing one's body (or those of others) (Gilligan, 2000, p.110).

Gilligan talks about the role of "culture" in violence:

> Gender codes reinforce the socialization of girls and women, socializing them to acquiesce in, support, defend, and cling to the traditional set of social roles, and to enforce conformity on other females as well.... Women are honoured for inactivity or passivity, for not engaging in forbidden activities. They are shamed or dishonoured if they are active where they should not be – sexually or in realms that are forbidden (professional ambition, aggressiveness, competitiveness and success, or violent activity, such as warfare or other forms of murder)... To speak of eliminating the sexual asymmetry that casts men and women into opposing sex roles is to speak of liberating both men and women from arbitrary and destructive stereotypes, and to begin treating both women and men as individuals, responding to their individual goals and abilities, rather than to the group (male or female) to which they belong (Gilligan, 2000, pp.229–233).

Gilligan writes that the enforced role of women as sex objects who are honoured when they conform and shamed when they rebel, has the consequence of encouraging men to treat them as sex objects and, indeed, incites violence in men because they feel "dishonoured" when women "transgress" their "prescribed role" (Gilligan, 2000, pp.229–233). It is worth noting here that Dr Parsey uses the word "seduced" with regard to Elizabeth's sexual encounter at the Great Exhibition. She may have been seduced, she may not.

How much of a part did powerlessness (a characteristic of poverty) play in Elizabeth's situation? Pierre Bourdieu, in his theory of "capital" claims that capital is power and that those without capital are powerless. Did Elizabeth's powerlessness contribute to her tragedy? Bourdieu describes capital as:

> accumulated labor (in its materialized form or its "incorporated" form) which, when appropriated on a private, i.e., exclusive, basis by agents or groups of agents, enables them to appropriate social energy in the form of reified or living labor... It is what makes the games of society – not least, the economic game – something other than simple games of chance offering at every moment the possibility of a miracle. Roulette, which holds out the opportunity of winning a lot of money in a short space of time, and therefore of changing one's social status quasi-instantaneously, and in which the winning of the previous spin of the wheel can be staked and lost at every new spin, gives a fairly accurate image of this imaginary universe of perfect competition or perfect equality of opportunity, a world without inertia, without accumulation, without heredity or acquired properties, in which every moment is perfectly independent of the previous one, every soldier has a marshal's baton in his knapsack, and every prize can be attained, instantaneously, by everyone, so that at each moment anyone can become anything (Bourdieu, 1986, pp.241–258).

Bourdieu goes on to explain how capital (or power) presents (paupers were devoid of all three types):

> Capital can present itself in three fundamental guises: as *economic capital,* which is immediately and directly convertible into money and may be institutionalized in the form of property rights; as *cultural capital,* which is convertible, in certain conditions, into economic capital and may be institutionalized in the form of educational qualifications; and as *social capital,* made up of social obligations ("connections"), which is convertible, in certain conditions, into economic capital and may be institutionalized in the form of a title of nobility (Bourdieu,1986, pp.241–58).

If it is true that eighty five percent of everything a child learns, s/he learns at home, Bourdieu's theory of cultural capital has huge ramifications for poor children. He says that

> Cultural capital can exist in three forms: in the *embodied* state, i.e., in the form of long-lasting dispositions of the mind and body; in the *objectified* state, in the form of cultural goods (pictures, books, dictionaries, instruments, machines, etc.), which are the trace or realization of theories or critiques of those theories, problematics, etc.; and in the *institutionalized* state, ... The notion of cultural capital initially presented itself to me,... as a theoretical hypothesis which made it possible to explain the unequal scholastic achievement of children originating from the different social classes by relating academic success, i.e., the specific profits which children from the different classes and class fractions can obtain in the academic market, to the distribution of cultural capital between the classes and class fractions... the scholastic yield from educational action depends on the cultural capital previously invested by the family. Moreover, the economic and social yield of the educational qualification depends on the social capital, again inherited, which can be used to back it up (Bourdieu, 1986, pp.241–258).

The analogy of the roulette table is so powerful because it shows so clearly how "trickle down" policies are inadequate in the efforts to make society more equal. What is more, according to Bourdieu,

> the initial accumulation of cultural capital, the precondition for the fast, easy accumulation of every kind of useful cultural capital, starts at the outset, without delay, without wasted time, only for the offspring of families endowed with strong cultural capital; in this case, the accumulation period covers the whole period of socialization (Bourdieu, 1986, pp.241–258.)

The various forms of capital combine to amplify their efficacy and force, and Bourdieu denotes the effect they have on the "value" of people:

> the share in profits which scarce cultural capital secures in class-divided societies is based, in the last analysis, on the fact that all agents do not have the economic and cultural means for prolonging their children's education beyond the minimum necessary for the reproduction of the labor-power least valorized at a given moment (Bourdieu,1986, pp.241–258).

Elizabeth was indeed experiencing powerlessness and vulnerability as a Victorian woman and a pauper, and another way of understanding her situation might be the Political Economy Approach:

> The "Political Economy Approach" sees power as the ability to command control over resources, and may be especially useful for conceptualising 'powerlessness' as well as power. According to a political economy approach, vulnerability should be understood in terms of powerlessness rather than simply material need or the failure of basic 'entitlements'. Power and powerlessness determine the distribution of access to food and other key commodities and assets among and within different groups. Those who lack power

> cannot safeguard their basic political, economic and social rights, and may not be able to protect themselves from violence. Vulnerability and power are therefore analysed as a political and economic process, in terms, for instance, of neglect, exclusion or exploitation, in which a variety of groups and actors play a part ((Collinson 2003:10) Gaventa, 2003, p16).

What would happen now in a similar situation? A modern-day Elizabeth would be very likely detained in hospital under S.37 of The Mental Health Act 1983:

> 37 – (1) Where a person is convicted before the Crown Court of an offence punishable with imprisonment other than an offence the sentence for which is fixed by law, or is convicted by a magistrates' court of an offence punishable on summary conviction with imprisonment, and the conditions mentioned in subsection (2) below are satisfied, the court may by order authorise his admission to and detention in such hospital as may be specified in the order or, as the case maybe, place him under the guardianship of a local social services authority or of such other person approved by a local social services authority as may be so specified..... (2) The conditions referred to in subsection (1) above are that – (a) the court is satisfied, on the written or oral evidence of two registered medical practitioners, that the offender is suffering from [mental disorder] and that either – (i) the mental disorder from which the offender is suffering is of a nature or degree which makes it appropriate for him to be detained in a hospital for medical treatment and [appropriate medical treatment is available for him]; or (ii) in the case of an offender who has attained the age of 16 years, the mental disorder is of a nature or degree which warrants his reception into guardianship under this Act; and (b) the court is of the opinion, having regard to all the circumstances including the nature of the offence and the character and

> antecedents of the offender, and to the other available methods of dealing with him, that the most suitable method of disposing of the case is by means of an order under this section (Jones, 2011, pp.223-224).

The origins of section 37 may be ultimately based on the case against James Hadfield (see Chapter 1).

> Once the offender is admitted to hospital pursuant to a hospital order or transfer order without restriction on discharge, his position is almost exactly the same as if he were a civil patient. In effect he passes out of the penal system and into the hospital regime. Neither the court nor the Secretary of State has any say in his disposal. Thus, like any other mental patient, he may be detained only for a period of six months, unless the authority to detain is renewed, an event which cannot happen unless certain conditions, which resemble those which were satisfied when he was admitted, are fulfilled. If the authority expires without being renewed the patient may leave. Furthermore, he may be discharged at any time by the hospital managers or the "responsible clinician"... (Jones, 2011, p.226).

If the present day Elizabeth had ongoing mental health difficulties, she could receive support and supervision under section 41 after discharge. Pertaining to sections 3 and 37, under s 117 of the Act the modern-day Elizabeth would be entitled to receive after-care if she needed it:

> (2) It shall be the duty of the [Primary Care Trust or] [Local Health Board] and of the local social services authority to provide, in co-operation with relevant voluntary agencies, after-care services for any person to whom this section applies until such time as the [Primary Care Trust or] [Local Health Board] and the local social services authority are satisfied that the person concerned is no

> longer in need of such services... (Jones, 2011, p.466).

The point of after-care is to help maintain the person's mental health in the best possible state, and therefore avoid the distress of further admissions to hospital. In 1852 after-care did not exist and Elizabeth is discharged and left to get on with her life as best she can.

As for the present day, how are mental health services shaping up for women? Nothing comes out of vacuum. Mental health care can only ever be a reflection of the society in which it is placed. The oppression of women and girls remains very present in modern day society. A visit to a psychiatric ward will usually reveal a majority of female patients, many of whom have experienced childhood sexual abuse. There are now many women working in the service, which is favourable in comparison with Victorian times, but the managers of those services are still disproportionately male, and they are the ones who commission services. It is not that men cannot respond to women's needs and problems empathically – they can and often do - but in order for society to really change, a sea-change needs to happen at the top. Moreover, Susie Orbach and Luise Eichenbaum make a strong case for feminist orientated therapy for individual women.

> The simultaneous but more subtle, and frequently unconscious, ways in which the mother-daughter relationship guides our taking up our gendered positions is of principal concern to us in coming to grips with understanding women's inner experience. The way in which the mothering person presents the psychological possibilities that exist are shaped by many factors. They include the mother's own experience of being mothered, they rest on her conscious and unconscious feelings about having a daughter, her identification with a same-sexed child, and they are influenced by the kind of support she receives in parenting, and her own internal object relations. All of these factors are framed within the social matrix of the mother, who as a member of the subordinate sex is charged with bringing up her daughter to assume a similar social

> position... It is an ironic and cruel phenomenon of patriarchy that the already oppressed shall prepare the succeeding generation for a similar fate (Ernst and Maguire, 1987, pp.58–59).

As Orbach and Eichenbaum also point out, women and girls are socialised to put the needs of others' first, often to the detriment of their own.

> In the past, and to a lesser extent at present, there was a lack of awareness and/or acknowledgment that women constitute an oppressed group in our culture. For some women, greater equity in both the personal and the political, or the private and public, spheres of their lives has led to positive experiences of mental health throughout their life. Yet to 'have it all' – that is, to obtain a good education, work and for many also run a home and have families, often brings its own stress. As Barnes & Maple (1992) comment, for many women the reality of employment both inside and outside the home means working in excess of 70 hours per week, and average of 11 hours a week more than male counterparts (Thompson and Mathias, 2003, p.375).

In the situation of a woman experiencing post-partum psychosis who had not killed one of her babies, the race would be on, in the present day, to try to find a bed at a Mother and Baby Unit (MBU). She might need to be detained under s.2 of The Mental Health Act if her behaviour was presenting risks to her own safety or that of others or even one of the emergency sections such as s. 4 (based on the recommendation of one doctor lasting for seventy-two hours) or s. 5, (a "holding power" for a patient who is already a voluntary patient in hospital which also lasts for seventy-two hours), but "sectioning" is not an end in itself. A care pathway is needed and an idea of the best treatment for that woman and her family. According to Action on Postpartum Psychosis (APP), there are only fifteen MBUs (111 beds in total) in the UK (there are none in Wales). "Of the 40,000 who have antenatal or postnatal problems, or both, only a quarter get access to specialist perinatal mental health services" (Siddique, 2016, p.4). If no MBU beds are available, the mother would need to be admitted to the nearest psychiatric hospital which has a bed available, and the baby would need to be cared for at home separating mother and child, which is not helpful.

> "I had postpartum psychosis. More must be done to help mothers like me. Postnatal depression's bigger, uglier brother hit me. When all eyes are on the beautiful baby, we can forget to look at the mum." (Leclerc, 2014,).

Chapter 5

JENNIFER

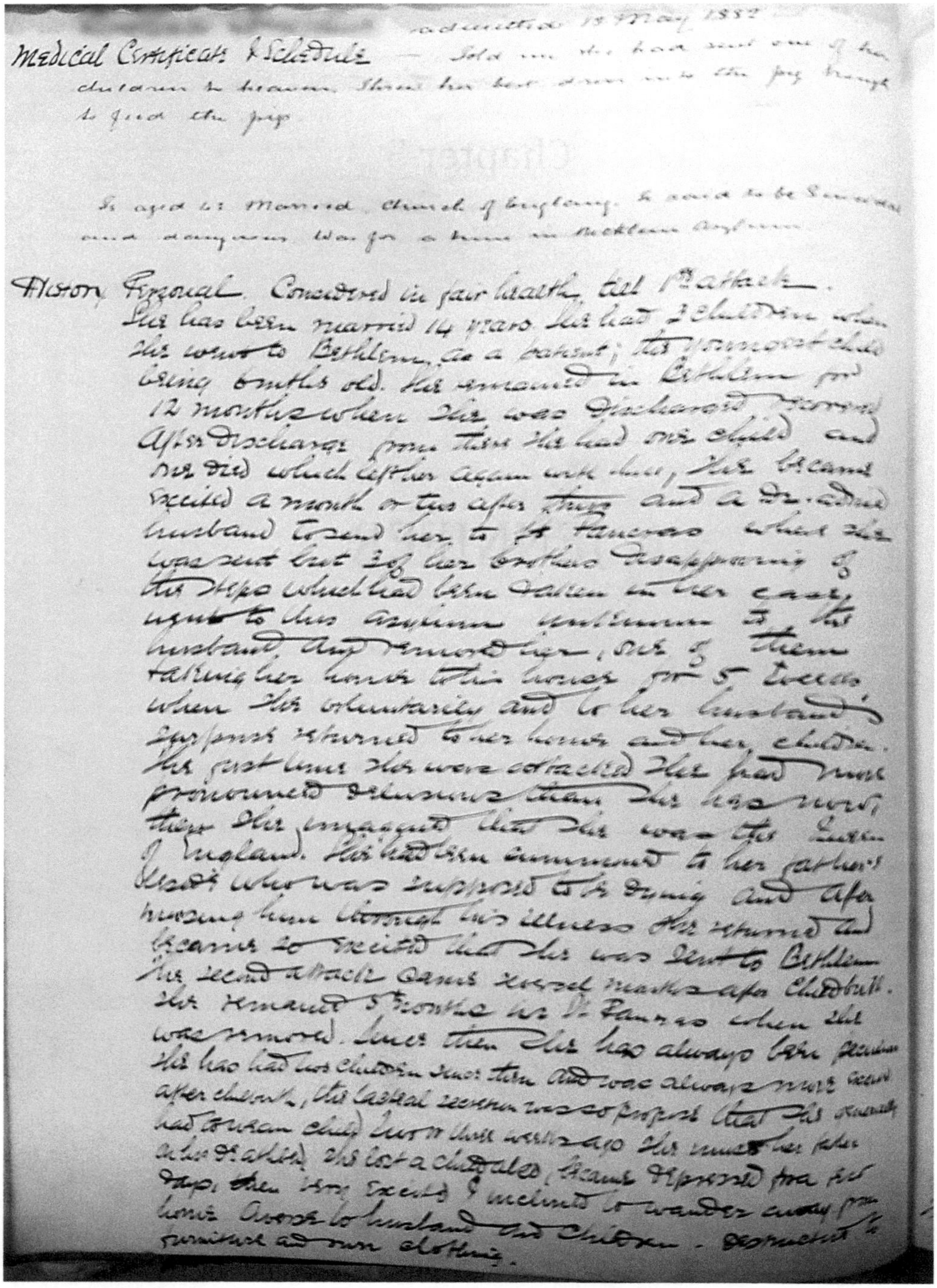

admitted 18 May 1882

Medical Certificate & Schedule — Said ... she had sent one of her children to heaven. Threw her best dress into the pig trough to feed the pigs.

Is aged 42 Married, Church of England. Is said to be Suicidal and dangerous. Was for a time in Bethlem Asylum

History Personal. Considered in fair health till 1st attack. She has been married 14 years. She had 3 children when she went to Bethlem as a patient; the youngest child being 6 mths old. She remained in Bethlem for 12 months when she was discharged recovered. After discharge from there she had one child and one died which left her again with three, she became excited a month or two after this and a Dr. advised husband to send her to St Pancras where she was sent but 3 of her brothers disapproving of the steps which had been taken in her case, went to this asylum unknown to the husband and removed her, one of them taking her home to his house for 5 weeks, when she voluntarily and to her husband's surprise returned to her home and her children. The first time she was attacked she had more pronounced delusions than she has now, there she imagined that she was the Queen of England. She had been summoned to her father's bedside who was supposed to be dying and after nursing him through his illness she returned and became so excited that she was sent to Bethlem. The second attack came several months after childbirth. She remained 5 months in St Pancras when she was removed. Since then she has always been peculiar. She has had two children since then and was always more [illegible] after childbirth, the latest [illegible] was so [illegible] that she had to wean child [illegible] three weeks ago she [illegible] her father [illegible] she lost a child aged [illegible], became depressed for a few days, then very excited & inclined to wander away from home. Averse to husband and children. Destructive to furniture and own clothing.

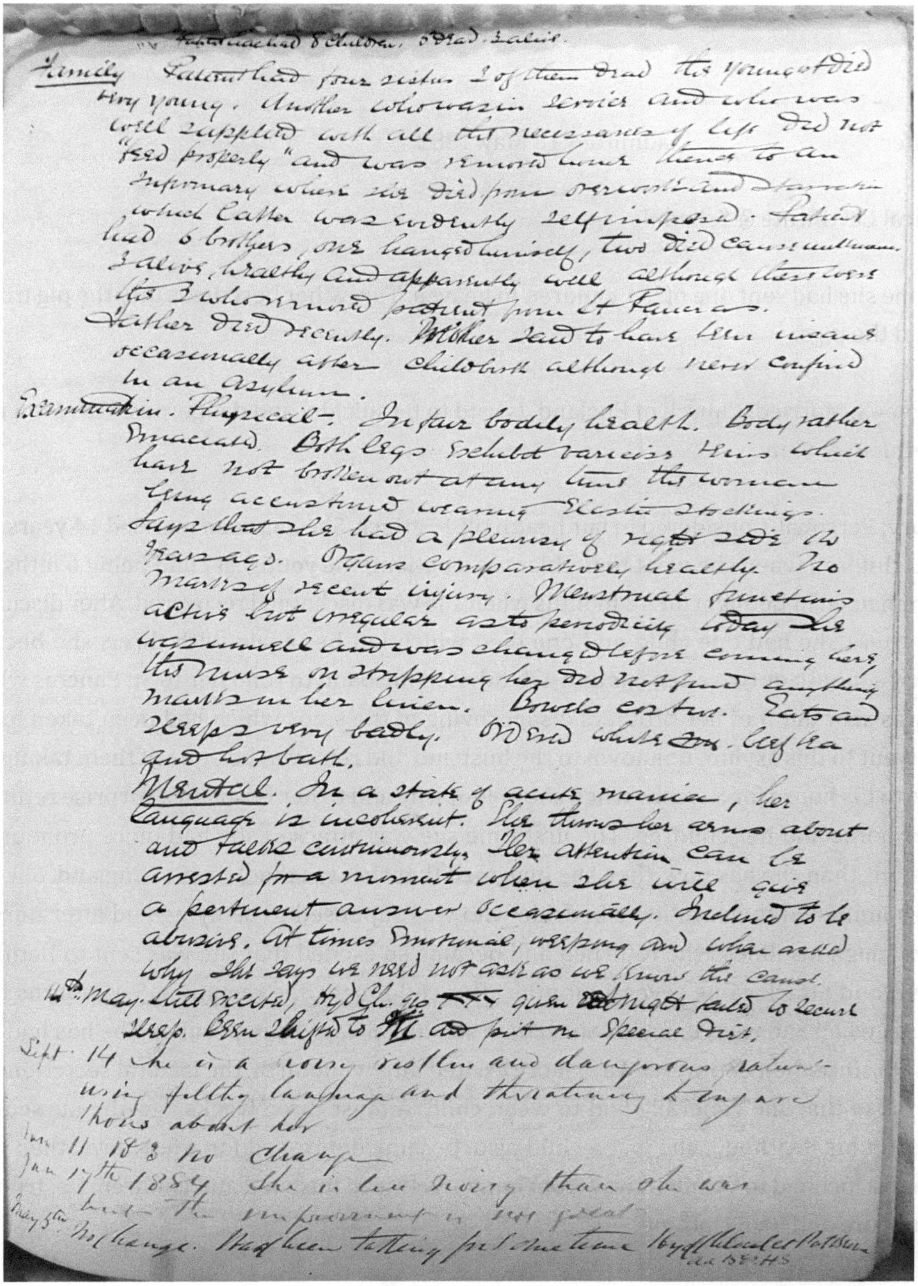

" [illegible] had 8 children, 6 dead 2 alive.

Family. Patient had four sisters 2 of them dead the youngest died very young. Another who was in service and who was well supplied with all the necessaries of life did not "feed properly" and was removed home thence to an Infirmary where she died from [illegible] and starvation which latter was evidently self imposed. Patient had 6 brothers, one hanged himself, two died cause unknown. 3 alive, healthy and apparently well although these were the 3 who removed patient from St Pancras. Father died recently. Mother said to have been insane occasionally after childbirth although never confined in an asylum.

Examination. Physical. In fair bodily health. Body rather emaciated. Both legs exhibit varicose veins which have not broken out at any time the woman being accustomed wearing elastic stockings. Says that she had a pleurisy of right side [illegible] years ago. Organs comparatively healthy. No marks of recent injury. Menstrual functions active but irregular as to periodicity today she was unwell and was changed before coming here, the nurse on stripping her did not find anything marks on her linen. Bowels costive. Eats and sleeps very badly. Ordered whisky [illegible]. beef tea and hot bath.

Mental. In a state of acute mania, her language is incoherent. She throws her arms about and talks continuously. Her attention can be arrested for a moment when she will give a pertinent answer occasionally. Inclined to be abusive. At times emotional, weeping and when asked why she says we need not ask as we know the cause.

14th May. Still excited, Hyd Chl. gr [illegible] given tonight failed to secure sleep. Been shifted to [illegible] and put on special diet.

Sept. 14 She is a noisy restless and dangerous patient using filthy language and threatening to injure those about her

Jan 11 1883 No change

Jan 17th 1884 She is less noisy than she was but the improvement is not great

May 5th No change. Had been talking for some time [illegible]

Opposite and above: Ref: CR 1664/652

Chapter 5: Jennifer

Jennifer admitted 13 May 1882

Medical Certificate & Schedule

Told me she had sent one of her children to heaven. Threw her best dress into the pig trough to feed the pigs.

Is aged 43. Married. Church of England. Is said to be suicidal and dangerous. Was for a time in Bethlem Asylum.

History: Personal. Considered in fair health till 1st attack. She has been married 14 years. She had 3 children when she went to Bethlem as a patient; the youngest child being 6 mths old. She remained in Bethlem for 12 months when she was discharged recovered. After discharge from there she had one child and one died which left her again with three, she became excited a month or two after this and a dr advised husband to send her to St. Pancras where she was sent but 3 of her brothers disapproving of the steps which had been taken in her case went to this asylum unknown to the husband and removed her, one of them taking her home to his house for 5 weeks when she voluntarily and to her husband's surprise returned to her home and her children. The first time she was attacked she had more pronounced delusions than she has now, then she imagined that she was the Queen of England. She had been summoned to her father's bedside who was supposed to be dying and after nursing him through his illness she returned and became so excited that she was sent to Bethlem. The second attack came several months after childbirth. She remained 5 + months in St Pancras when she was removed. Since then she has always been peculiar. She has had two children since then and was always more excited after childbirth, the lacteral secretion was so profuse that she generally had to wean child. Almost three weeks ago she nursed her father on his deathbed, she lost a child also, became depressed for a few days, then very excited & inclined to wander away from home. Averse to husband and children. Destructive to furniture and own clothing.

Patient has had 8 children. 5 dead, 3 alive

<u>Family</u>. Patient had 4 sisters 2 of them dead, the youngest died very young. Another who was in service and who was well supplied with all the necessaries of life did not "feed properly" and was removed home thence to an infirmary where she died from overwork and starvation which latter was evidently self-imposed. Patient had 6 brothers, one hanged himself, two died cause unknown, 3 alive, healthy and apparently well although these were the three who removed patient from St Pancras. Father died recently. Mother said to have been insane occasionally after childbirth although never confined in an asylum.

Examination: Physical:- In fair bodily health. Body rather emaciated. Both legs exhibit varices [sic] veins those which have not broken out at any time the woman being accustomed {to} wearing elastic stockings. Says that she had a pleurisy of right side 12 years ago. Organs comparatively healthy. No marks of recent injury. Menstrual functions active but irregular as to periodicity. Today she was unwell and was changed before coming here, the nurse on stripping her did not find anything [sic] marks in her linen. Bowels costive. Eats and sleeps very badly, ordered white leaf tea and hot bath.

<u>Mental:-</u> In a state of acute mania, her language is incoherent. She throws her arms about and talks continuously. Her attention can be arrested for a moment when she will give a pertinent answer occasionally. Inclined to be abusive. At times emotional, weeping and when asked why, she says we need not ask as we know the cause.

14th May Still excited, Hyd Ch q xxx given at night failed to secure sleep. Been shifted to M and put on special diet.

Sept 14 She is a noisy, restless and dangerous patient using filthy language and threatening to injure those about her.

Jan 11 1883 No change.

Jan 17 1884 She is less noisy than she was but the improvement is not great.

May 5th No change. Had been taking for some time {? Chloral Hydrate} et Potassium."

{Chloral Hydrate given as a sedative.}

Looking at the Census of 1851, we find Jennifer's birth family at South Hackney: T, 39, Gardener from Hackney (head); M, 36, Laundress from Suffolk (wife); T, 14; J, 13; {Jennifer}, 12; M 10; J, 8; H, 5; F, 1. In June 1866 Jennifer marries J E (bachelor) at the parish church in South Hackney. In the 1871 Census the couple are lodging at St Mary le Bow (there are two children; D, 4, and A who is 1). By 1881 they have moved to Rugby, and D has died. It is worth noting here that Jennifer's admission to Hatton was in 1882 (the year following that Census), but that her first admission to hospital in London had been three and a half years before. The next Census entry is significant and could offer one explanation for Jennifer's mental distress and explain why her three brothers discharged her from St Pancras hospital, without informing her husband. In 1891 J E, Railway Guard from Dymchurch, Kent is living at St Pancras, London and living with him is M (Jennifer's younger sister) who is described as "single, 50, and Housekeeper from South Hackney (cousin)". Jennifer never left the Asylum and died on 22nd October 1905 in Hatton aged 66. In the records she is described as "married, housewife" and the apparent cause of death "congestion of lungs (chronic mania)" (CR 1664/516). In October 1906, J E and M marry in London.

It is not difficult to empathise with Jennifer when we see written in her notes "at times emotional, weeping and when asked why, she says we need not ask as we know the cause." The written history is confusing, unempathetic, and leaves us with many questions. It appears that Jennifer was living with bipolar disorder (please see Chapter 2 for information) and that there is a significant family history of mental illness/distress (including anorexia nervosa?) and suicide; there is an overwhelming amount of loss (five children and siblings as well as her father). (Doubly poignant (for us reading about her now) is the possibility that more of Jennifer's children might have survived if she had not weaned them due to the 'profuseness' of her breast milk.) There are many births (which may well have been difficult) and many child deaths, which must have been traumatic. There are queries about the happiness of her marriage. Why did her three brothers act in unison to remove Jennifer from hospital, without informing J E, and take her home with them? It says in the notes that Jennifer is "averse" to her husband (not surprising if he was having a relationship with her younger sister and Jennifer knew about it), but why then did she return to the marital home? We shall never know for sure. The doctor seems to query the sanity of the three brothers who removed Jennifer from St Pancras Hospital, but they may well have had good reason (the Census throws up a possible explanation), and they seem to have acted together. Had J E placed her in the asylum to get her out of the way? When did J E's relationship with M begin, how much did Jennifer know and how much did her brothers know? Jennifer may have known (or suspected) for some time that her husband and her sister were closer than they should be. It would have been a scandal if known about publicly and Jennifer would have felt shame, humiliation and anger about it, but not have been able to discuss her feelings openly. It doesn't appear that staff at the hospital knew about J E and M.

Jennifer's discharge from St Pancras at the request of her brothers brings up some interesting questions regarding the role of the nearest relative in a patient's care.

> The origins of the nearest relative (NR) might, perhaps, be found in the Act for Regulating Private Madhouses, which was introduced in 1774. It required that private madhouses be licensed, and introduced a process of certification for all but pauper lunatics. Crucially, the Act also said that, alongside the name of the advising physician or apothecary, the admission certificate should bear the name of the person committing the patient to confinement. That person was often a relative (Hewitt, 2011, p.13).

Now, Jennifer was a pauper, so appears not to have been eligible for/afforded those rights. However, as we have seen in Chapter 1, abuses of power did occur. Rogers and Pilgrim write about the law acting in the interests of the third party (here J E and M) and it is very much to the point:

> The law has been used in a double and arguably contradictory way.

> On the one hand it has been a way of ensuring social order and is thus directed at controlling the deviant conduct associated with mental abnormality. On the other hand, it has also been used as a break on professional power. The State then *both* delegates powers of control and discretion to what we now call 'mental health professionals' *and* then operates to limit those powers. A further ambiguity has been that the State apparatus of legalism might be viewed as being inherently about third-party interests (those who are sane by common consent) against the interests of patients. Alternatively, it might be depicted as a means to protect the rights of the latter, including the right to treatment (Rogers and Pilgrim, 2014, p.158).

What would be the situation now, if Jennifer was to be assessed and detained under the Mental Health Act 1983? The "nearest relative" role in the Mental Health Act is a very important one, and it is a complex subject. I am only going to touch on aspects of it that are pertinent to Jennifer's situation here. In some ways the nearest relative has similar powers to the AMHP.

> He may make an application for assessment (section 2), an emergency application for admission (section 4) and an application for admission for treatment (section 3). No application for admission or treatment under section 3 may be made by an {approved mental health professional} (AMHP) without first consulting with the nearest relative unless the {AMHP} considers that such consultation is not reasonably practicable or would involve unreasonable delay (section 11(4)). The manager of a psychiatric institution in which a patient is detained has to inform the nearest relative in writing about, amongst other things, the right to apply to a tribunal, the right to be discharged, the right to receive and send correspondence and the right to consent to or refuse treatment (section 132(4)). A nearest relative may order the discharge of a patient who is detained under {section 2 and

> section 3 (section 23)}. Prior to exercising this important power the nearest relative can appoint a medical practitioner to examine the patient and the appointed practitioner can require the production of records relating to the detention or treatment of the patient (section 24). The right to order discharge under section 23 is limited when the {responsible clinician} certifies that the patient would, if released, be likely to be a danger to himself or others (section 25). Where a patient is to be discharged other than by the order of the nearest relative, the detaining authority is required to notify the nearest relative of the forthcoming discharge unless the patient requests that no such information is supplied (section 133(2)) (Jones, 2011, p.183).

It is important to note here, that the nearest relative can veto the detention of a person under s. 3 if they do not agree. The nearest relative is required to act on behalf of the patient, receiving information on behalf of the patient as to her/his rights and treatment while s/he is ill, and ensure that her/his rights are protected.

> In addition to the power to order a discharge under section 23 the nearest relative may apply to {a tribunal} for the discharge of the patient pursuant to section 66 ... Where the nearest relative is the applicant to the Tribunal he may appoint a registered medical practitioner to visit and examine the patient and that practitioner may require production of and inspect any records relating to the detention and treatment of the patient (section 76(1)) (Jones, 2011, p.183).

How is the nearest relative's status identified?

> 1.16 The identity of the nearest relative is to be determined according to criteria contained in section 26 of MHA 1983. Thus, a patient's spouse or civil partner will ordinarily take precedence

> over all other candidates. However, the criteria are complex: a spouse or civil partner might, for example, be overreached by the patient's child, parent or sibling, and all of them might be trumped by someone with whom the patient has been residing. There are strict rules governing who qualifies for the role of the nearest relative under the Act. There is a definition of 'relative' and 'nearest relative' in The Mental Health Act Manual 1–363, (s.26) (Jones, 2011, p.181).

Under the provisions of s.26 MHA 1983 Jennifer's nearest relative might well be her husband J E, (if she was residing with him at the time) and her brothers would have no legal right to discharge her. If, however, she had been living with one of her brothers prior to admission (rather than on discharge), or that brother had been providing her with care, that brother might become her nearest relative. This is because any relative with whom the patient "ordinarily resides" or gives 'more than minimal' care to the patient jumps to the top of the list as far as eligibility as nearest relative is concerned.

> In order to justify a finding that the relative is caring for the patient, the services provided by the relative must be more than minimal and they need not have been provided over the long term. In this case the court was asked {in Re D (Mental patient: habeas corpus) [200] 2 F.L.R. 848} to consider the situation of a relative who assisted the patient in managing his financial affairs, checked whether he was eating appropriately and took away and cleaned his soiled clothing and bed clothes. In finding that the relative was caring for the patient the court said that there "was more than sufficient evidence to pass the 'cared for' test, wherever one sets the threshold of services amounting to 'cared for'. In other words, the services were not merely minimal. They were services which were substantial and sustained (Jones, 2011, p.187).

The nearest relative is, in fact, required to act in the patient's best interests while that patient is mentally ill. Lord Hunt, the then Health Minister, clarified the duty of the nearest relative role:

> "Of course, many people chosen by the patient would feel duty-bound to act in the way that the patient wished, but the powers of the nearest relative have not been designed to work in that way. […] Given the role, the nearest relative needs to be able to act, as I said, in a way that represents their understanding of the patient's best interest and not simply to carry out the patient's wishes."

The nearest relative has several powers conferred by the MHA. While nearly all applications for admission under the MHA are made by an Approved Mental Health Professional (AMHP), the nearest relative can apply (section 11 MHA). However, in practice this option is exercised very rarely (Jones, 2013, p.86).

One of the reasons for this is so that the patient cannot claim at a later date that their relative has 'sectioned' them as the decision to apply is not usually made by the nearest relative but by an AMHP with a more professionally detached 'objective' view of the patient and their circumstances. The AMHP has a duty to inform the nearest relative that an application might be made or has been made (section 11 MHA) but it is the decision of the AMHP and the assessing Doctors as to whether the patient is admitted to hospital and not the nearest relatives. The AMHP's duty is to consult and not necessarily to agree with the preference the relative states. Jones (2013, p.89) cites, The consultation will have two objectives. The first will be to provide information to the AMHP to assist with the decision of whether to apply for admission. The second will be to put the nearest relative in a position to object to an application (Smith, 2015, p.340).

What if the selection of the nearest relative would be a potential cause for concern regarding potential abuse or emotional distress to the patient? This is a question that might well be relevant to Jennifer's situation. (The nearest relative assumes a big role, after all, in the patient's care.) What then? Prior to the MHA 2007 amendments,

> 1.17 Crucially, the section 26 criteria are fixed and inflexible, and they do not afford a patient any role in the determining of his or her nearest relative. As a result, a patient might find him- or herself with a nearest relative whom he or she neither approves of nor wants (Hewitt, 2011, p.16–17).

Imagine the potential distress inflicted on Jennifer, if we are correct in our surmises about the state of her relationship with her husband, if J E (or, indeed, M) was her nearest relative under the Act! There were two legal challenges to the provisions regarding the selection of the nearest relative in 1999 and 2000 when the Government conceded that Article 8 of the ECHR had been breached. Then in 2005

> The Government's failure to reconcile the nearest relative provisions in MHA 1983 with the ECHR led some practitioners to adopt makeshift solutions of their own. One such was revealed in the case of *R (E) v. Bristol City Council*, which came before the High Court in January 2005.
>
> 1.26 At the heart of this case was the requirement, contained in section 11(4) of MHA 1983, that before making an application for a patient's detention under section 3, an Approved Social Worker (ASW) (the forerunner of the Approved Mental Health Professional (AMHP)) should consult his or her nearest relative. No such consultation need take place, however, if it is "not reasonably practicable" (Hewitt, 2011, pp.19–20).

Hewitt goes on to describe an important case (R (E) v. Bristol City Council) which highlighted the problem. Under the MHA 1983 E feared that in any future MHA assessment the acting ASW (now AMHP) would have to consult her sister (S) as her nearest relative. This would have added to her mental distress at a time of crisis, as E did not enjoy a good relationship with her sister. Under the Act though, the ASW would have to consult S. In legal proceedings the Judge agreed with E and under judicial review the High Court found in E's favour and it was stated that under Article 8 of the European Convention on Human Rights (ECHR) E had a right to a private life. The Court's decision was that the domestic authorities should be able to interpret the wording of the MHA – "not reasonably practicable" – in a way that was in E's favour. In short, the ASW was to make a judgement, using common sense with regard to consultation with the person in the nearest relative role, and not consult if that would cause added distress to the person being assessed (Hewitt, 2011, pp.19–20).

This is partly why in 2007 the MHA was amended to include the following provisions:

- A patient him- or herself may seek the appointment of an acting nearest relative.

- A patient may apply to discharge, or to vary an order appointing an acting nearest relative.

- There is a further ground for displacement: the nearest relative of the patient is 'not a suitable person to act as such' (Hewitt, 2011, pp.24-25).

It does happen, of course, that patients feel resentment towards their relatives (and indeed the AMHP) when they have been detained. Service users detained under the MHA are after all, by definition, unwilling service users, not 'customers' with choice.

> As Campbell puts it, 'Numerous recipients of crisis services are not just unwilling recipients but are compelled recipients' (Read & Reynolds, 2000, p 180). The fact that there is this *involuntary* aspect to being forced to use services, or having services 'forced' upon them, is a significant feature here. By definition, people assessed under MHA have not asked for this to happen, as if they were thought to need hospital admission and had agreed to this they would become voluntary patients and thus avoid the need for formal assessment under the MHA. Similarly, most nearest relatives have not chosen or agreed to take this role. The role is determined for them by section 26 MHA as outlined above. Therefore the involuntary and possibly unwilling and compelled aspects of the role are inherent in it (Smith, 2015 p.343).

> Szasz (1963) has argued that as long as there is legislation authorizing compulsory detention there can be no genuine voluntary admission (Rogers and Pilgrim, 2014, p.166).

It is worth thinking about this in relation to mental health services and accessibility. Many Black, Asian and Minority Ethnic (BAME) service users complain, with justification, that mental health services are not sensitive to their needs or cultures, and this may at least partly explain why BAME service users are over-represented in the figures for detention under the MHA. BAME groups are not getting the kind of help they need early enough, and because of this they may become seriously mentally ill and need detention under the MHA.

> Last month's race disparity audit showed that common mental disorders such as anxiety and depression were most prevalent among black women, while black men were more than 10 times as likely to have experienced a psychotic disorder within the past year as white men. Yet the audit also showed that black adults in the general population were the least likely to report being in

> receipt of any treatment – medication, counselling or therapy, and the most likely to have been detained under the Mental Health Act. Dyer {Jacqui Dyer, appointed to the advisory panel for the government's review of the MHA} suggests the rate of detentions is linked to not enough people having access to early intervention services... Dyer says that black voices are rarely heard at the decision-making table, where more are needed, locally as well as nationally (Mulholland, 2017, p.3).

And yet the respect principle included in the Code of Practice to the MHA states:

> 4-013 1.4 People taking decisions under the Act must recognise and respect the diverse needs, values and circumstances of each patient, including their race, religion, culture, gender, age, sexual orientation and any disability. They must consider the patient's views, wishes and feelings (whether expressed at the time or in advance), so far as they are reasonably ascertainable, and follow those wishes wherever practicable and consistent with the purpose of the decision. There must be no unlawful discrimination (Jones, 2011, p.767).

Moreover,

> 4-014 1.5 Patients must be given the opportunity to be involved, as far as is practicable in the circumstances, in planning, developing and reviewing their own treatment and care to help ensure that it is delivered in a way that is as appropriate and effective for them as possible (Jones, 2011, pp.766–7).

There is evidence that the compulsory provisions of the MHA are being used more than strictly necessary, due to pressures on resources, and this is a distortion of the guiding principles of the Act: that compulsory detention should be a final resort, when all other avenues are closed.

> A lack of mental health services in England means a growing number of patients are having to be sectioned to get help, according to the NHS care regulator. A review by the Care Quality Commission found that the rise in the number of detentions under the Mental Health Act was due partly to the fact that the healthcare system was "under considerable strain". The number of patients sectioned has increased by 40% between 2005–06 and 2015–16, from 45,484 to 63,622. The CQC noted that unavailability of community care support was leading to high numbers of detentions, and demand for beds also meant patients tended not to be admitted on a voluntary basis. Dr Paul Lelliott, the lead for mental health at the Care Quality Commission, said: "Some of the factors at play in the rising rates of detention, both nationally and locally, are also signs of a healthcare system under considerable strain. Detentions under the act can be influenced by gaps in support and provision in the system." He added: "This includes limited hospital bed availability, which means that people cannot easily be admitted as voluntary patients early in the course of their illness" (Marsh, 2018, p.3).

Detention under the Act should be a last resort when all other forms of help have failed, not the only means to get a patient treatment. This arbitrary use of legislation will also affect the numbers of people who are becoming 'nearest relatives', and experiencing the responsibilities that can bring. What is more, the lack of bed availability is resulting in patients being sent to hospital many miles from home and family, making it difficult for families to offer support, and community staff to offer continuity of care. Moreover,

> The restriction on numbers of psychiatric beds may mean now that risky conduct, rather than expressed need, drives admission priorities, but that other means such as Community Treatment

> Orders (CTOs) will be used more (Rogers and Pilgrim, 2014, p.172).

What would be the options for care for Jennifer in the present day? She would be offered mood stabilising drugs and talking treatments; she would be able to divest J E of his role as nearest relative under the Act, and she might be subject to a Community Treatment Order (s.17), or Guardianship (s.7) under the Mental Health Act. She might well be eligible under s.117 for aftercare.

The AMHP's responsibility to interview the service user "in a suitable manner" and consult with the nearest relative during a Mental Health Act assessment, facilitates understanding of the situation, keeps communication open (without breaching confidentiality) and Smith (2015, p342) points out that

> Cameron and McGowan's (2013, p.27), {comment that} the social worker (AMHP in this case) can function as transitional participant 'who can usefully bridge and integrate the disparate aspects of the ... determined social (external) and subjective emotional (internal) environments of their clients". It is bridging these two aspects of experience that the AMHP is attempting when talking with nearest relatives (Smith, 2015, p.342).

Relatives play an important part in patient's lives, for good or ill:

> Whether or not psychiatric patients enter the role voluntarily or involuntarily, it is not unusual for their relatives (or 'significant others') to be interested parties with regard to service contact. Not only might they be involved in formal decision-making about hospital admission, they might have previously been involved in engendering, coping with, and eventually informally labelling the incipient patient's mental abnormality, prior to formal psychiatric diagnosis (Rogers and Pilgrim, 2014, p.202).

As Rogers and Pilgrim go on to say, relatives can act as visitors, carers, advocates and referrers. But as Jennifer's case illustrates, the situation can be complex.

> The concept of the 'betrayal funnel' first put forward by Goffman (1961), suggested that psychiatric coercion was used as a solution for those immediately around mad people to resolve a shared social crisis. This implied some sort of conscious or unconscious alliance of professionals and relatives against the patient. The prospect of this oppressive collusion triggered an unresolved debate about whether a relative should be construed as a 'carer', always acting beneficently for the patient, or as a beneficiary of actions that might be against the patient's interest (or even a variable mixture from case to case). The ambiguity is made more acute when the impact on the mental health of 'carers' is taken into consideration. This has sometimes been conceptualized as 'burden'. However, it is clear that 'burden' and therefore the likelihood of a carer developing a mental health problem themselves is more likely in the presence of significant unmet needs of the 'patient' (Cleary *et al.* 2006) (Rogers and Pilgrim, 2014, p.202).

The idea of "oppressive collusion" could be extremely pertinent to Jennifer's case, if we are reading the situation correctly. The writer of the Case History implies that her three brothers who discharged her might also be mentally ill for having done so. No-one appears to have asked them why they acted in the way they did.

> Hardcastle et al. (2007, p.78) show how relatives of mental health service users can feel guilt, fear, despair and anger. One father writes poignantly of his experience: "The worst thing that happened in my life was having my son admitted to hospital against his will ... The hardest thing I did was to help the police put

> handcuffs on him. It was the only way to help him at the time, but the memory of doing that will stay with me for the rest of my life … I 'phoned my wife. She couldn't stop crying, and I felt I needed to be there to support her, but wanted to find out what was happening. I felt really torn, feeling in need of support myself, but having so many people who needed my support … My son had lots of odd ideas about what had been going on in the weeks before he was admitted, some of them relating to other family members … I know we did not always come across as reasonable, but at the beginning we were in shock, and later on we couldn't understand what was happening. I would have thought they would have understood our emotions better…" (Hardcastle, 2007, pp.80–82)(Smith, 2015, p.345).

The AMHP needs to be able to listen to (and really 'hear') those involved in the crisis, that is partly what 'interviewing in a suitable manner' entails.

> While trends and fashions in social work and mental health thinking come and go, the essential needs of people in crisis have changed relatively little since earliest civilizations. Biesteck (1967, p.135) claims, 'All human beings have certain common basic needs: physical, emotional, intellectual, social and spiritual. In adverse circumstances these common needs are felt with a special poignancy' (Smith, 2015, p.351).

When we look at Jennifer's case notes, we see a very complicated picture and the potential aetiology of her mental illness is just as complex a hypothesis. Looking at her case study, we could postulate genetics, social circumstances, psychological, emotional and physical causes for her experiencing bipolar disorder, and it's quite possible that all of those are partly responsible for her illness.

There is a definite family history of mental illness. Jennifer's mother experienced periods of mental disorder following childbirth, but was never hospitalised. A sister died of what sounds like anorexia nervosa. One brother completed suicide. This family history could be the result of a combination of genetic disposition, family dysfunction and trauma.

> Research has shown that there is a genetic predisposition or loading to the development of depression (McGuffin & Katz 1989). Expressed another way, this means that first degree relatives of depressives have at least twice the risk of developing depression than do those in the general population. A genetic component has been further supported by studies showing that identical twins are more likely both to have a history of depression, compared with non-identical twins (McGuffin, Katz & Rutherford 1991) (Thompson and Mathias, 2003, p.12).

Patterns of dysfunction and abuse can be passed on through parenting style. Another explanation could be offered by psychoanalysis and Melanie Klein's theories about the 'depressive position' in Object Relations. Yet another explanation could be offered via Beck's ideas on Cognitive Behavioural Therapy and the negative thought processes that can be passed on inter-generationally. Social work theory would offer Systems theory. Freud's ideas about loss and depression might be applied. Any of these theories or all could be relevant.

There are three main perspectives with which to examine mental illness – psychological, social and physical, and often they are all relevant because human beings are complex. Within each of these perspectives there are again different theories and ideas as to how people's mental health/ill-health develops. For example, within the psychological field, we have theorists like Freud and the psychodynamic practitioners who came after him who adapted his ideas. Then there is the theory of 'behaviourism' "fundamentally, the behavioural approach to abnormality emphasizes that maladaptive behaviours, such as phobias, anxiety, depression, are *learned* and can thus be unlearned." (Thompson and Mathias, 2003, p.11). Beck developed his theory in 1976 with regard to the ways people think and how that affects their behaviour (Cognitive Behavioural Therapy) (Beck, A. 1976). The social perspective might include theories around inequality (something we have looked at in other chapters), the impact of stress (generalised anxiety has been linked to chronic environmental stress, for example), isolation and adverse childhood events (ACEs).

With regard to the physical perspective, it is clear from research that stroke victims often experience depression in the period of their recovery.

> Brain damage to the left hemisphere due, for example, to a stroke results in depression more often than does damage to the right hemisphere. In total, around 25% of those who have had strokes develop a major depressive disorder in the acute phase (Robinson et al 1986). Lesions in the frontal lobes of the brain in particular can produce depression (Thompson and Mathias, 2003, p.13).

New research is being carried out into the possibility that some forms of schizophrenia may be due to an immune system disease affecting the brain (Devlin, 2017,).

To complicate the picture further there is the idea about vulnerability and risk factors in the development of mental illness: "those parts of the individual's physical, psychological or social make-up that lead to an increased vulnerability to the disorder in question" (Thompson and Mathias, 2003, p.12). Brown and Harris (1978) describe risk factors for developing depression among a group of women in a south London community. They thought of these risk factors as vulnerabilities (the loss of a mother before the age of 11; the absence of a confiding relationship; unemployment; the presence of three or more children at home; poor self-esteem). Brown and Harris also found that a precipitating factor in the more recent time was likely to cause the actual onset of the depression (eg the breakdown of a relationship) and that there were then maintaining factors which maintained the depression. If we apply this thesis to Jennifer's case, we could hypothesise that a vulnerability factor sustained in childhood might have been (for example) the loss of a sibling, or childhood neglect or abuse; a precipitating factor might have been (for example) the loss of a child she gave birth to (five of her children died) or her husband's infidelity with her sister; and a maintaining factor might be the shame she experienced because of her husband and sister's relationship and which prevented her from talking about it openly. Of course, the lack of a confiding relationship brings us full circle to isolation. Isolation and its dangers have been discussed in chapter 2. The importance of helping people to build good supportive relationships seems absolutely crucial within mental health work.

> It is a human-to-human relationship that can provide the acceptance, affirmation, respect and connection which can be key to reclaiming one's identity and place in the world (Holley, 2007) (Tew, 2011, p.14).

The "either/or" approach to explaining mental illness/distress (medical model versus the social model) seems inadequate, and as Tew explains:

> A rejection of the disease model of 'mental illness' does not imply that the biological dimension is unimportant. Far from it. However, a different model of causality may be required. Instead of some underlying illness being seen as the cause, and experiences of mental distress as symptoms, we are gaining increasing evidence that trauma and other adverse life experiences make their imprint on our physiology and biochemistry – and developments in brain-imaging technology are demonstrating just how much brain functioning may change in response to such experiences (Perry et al., 1995; Shonkoff and Phillips, 2000). In this way, the social can be the underlying cause *both* of problematic cognitive, emotional and behavioural responses *and* of associated biochemical and physiological changes. Alongside this, new experiences – either arising through therapy or exposure to more positive social situations – can lead to positive changes in brain functioning (Roffman et al., 2005) (Tew, 2011, p.26).

It may well be that our different genetic make-up and up-bringing affect our ability both to experience and cope with stress. Tew goes further:

> Nor does moving away from the 'illness' model of mental distress take away from the possibility that psychoactive medication can have specific effects (for example to tranquillise, to raise mood, or to distance a person from their emotions) which may or may not be helpful to people if they are experiencing mental distress. However, despite the impression created by pharmaceutical advertising, their action is not about targeting and curing particular 'illness' processes; instead they may be seen to act on anyone, irrespective of diagnosis, as do other psychoactive drugs such as sleeping pills or alcohol (Moncrieff, 2008). Thus, a revisioning of medical approaches would suggest that 'medication could be better targeted at problems and processes rather than putative "illnesses" '(Kinderman et al., 2008) – and the fact that someone may find medication helpful in enabling them to deal with their mental experience would not imply that they are suffering from any underlying brain disease (Tew, 2011, p.26).

Mental distress causes people difficulties within the areas of emotion, thinking and behaviour. In other words, that person's complete world. That can be seen very clearly in Jennifer's case. It really is true to say that there is no health without good mental health.

"What it's like to live with Bipolar II disorder" (Hawken, 2014).

Conclusion

This book used materials and documentation from the Central Hospital (Hatton Asylum) stored at Warwick Record Office. Being over one hundred years' old they are available for public viewing. Looking at them now, with the eye of a professional social worker, it is uncomfortably clear how little, in many ways, life has changed as far as adversity is concerned. Harold, growing up in a dysfunctional family; Arthur coping with bipolar disorder; Edith, so poor that she is unable to meet her needs; Elizabeth shamed by a discriminating society and Jennifer made vulnerable by her background and then betrayed by those she loved. What is more, all of these patients had families. How did their experiences impact them? All of these scenarios happen today, and perhaps mental 'illness' or distress will simply keep on presenting itself within people's lives.

Helping children develop resilience is one important way forward, along with policies (and funding) which seek to eliminate inequality and childhood abuse and neglect. Parenting support and education seems to be an essential, if as a society we are to lessen the vulnerabilities to mental illness. Resilience developed in childhood will lessen the impact of any precipitating factor. The movement towards a more open discussion about mental health and distress can only be a good thing, and will hopefully reduce that other great stumbling block – stigma.

In this book we have looked, in detail, at real people's medical notes and discussed some of the issues that present themselves within them. We compared the relevant treatments, legalities, contemporary social issues, with how they would be now. This helps to put mental health care in context and would be impossible to do with present-day patients for confidentiality reasons. It's very difficult to hear anyone's voice in the historical notes. We're told that Edith feels as though she has a mouse running around in her head, and we have one sad quote from Jennifer. One gets the impression that each patient was just a small cog in an enormous machine. I have wondered how they would feel if they knew that they were being written (and read) about in the present day. I hope to have magnified their significance a little.

With the perspective allowed us when we look back at another time, some injustices and inappropriate responses become glaringly obvious. I hope that, having read this book, students will feel better prepared for their placement, and that they will ask themselves some pertinent questions about care and control in the present day. For example: what is being done now that may well cause future generations to shake their heads in reproach?

Bibliography

Altick, R. (1990) *The Presence of the Present – Topics of the Day in the Victorian Novel.* Ohio State University Press

Armstrong, J. (2015) 'More than 80 suicide cases directly linked to Coalition cuts claim disability campaigners'. *Mirror Online* Available at: http://www.mirror.co.uk/news/uk-news/more-80-suicide-cases-directly-5634404

Ayre, D. (2016) 'Poor Mental Health. The links between child poverty and mental health problems'. *The Children's Society.*

BBC, (2015) 'More than 2,300 died after fit for work assessment – DWP figures'. Available at: www.bbc.co.uk?news/uk-34074557

Beck, A. T (1976) *Cognitive Therapy and the Emotional Disorders.* International Universities Press.

Bly, M. (2017) 'Jacob Rees-Mogg thinks food banks are 'uplifting'. For me, they're a necessity.' *The Guardian*

Bly, N. (1887) *Ten Days in a Mad-House*. Poland. Amazon Fulfillment

Bourdieu, P. (1986) 'The Forms of Capital' in Richardson, J. *Handbook of Theory and Research for the Sociology of Education.* (1986) Westport, CT: Greenwood.

Bronfenbrenner, U. (1992) 'Ecological Systems Theory', in Vasta, R (ed.) *Six Theories of Child Development. Revised Formulation and Current Issues,* Jessica Kingsley Publishers, London and Philadelphia

Brown, B. (2012) *Daring Greatly. How the Courage to be Vulnerable Transforms the Way We Live, Love, Parent and Lead.* Penguin Life. Random House, UK

Brown, G. and Harris, T. (1978) *The Social Origins of Depression.* London: Tavistock

Butler, P. (2017) 'Destitution is back. And we can't just ignore it.' *The Guardian,*

Cadwalladr, C. (2009) 'How Bridgend was damned by distortion', *The Observer.* https://www.theguardian.com/lifeandstyle/2009/mar/01/bridgend-wales-youth-suicide-media-ethics

Carson, G. (2018) Adults, Workforce. Community Care https://www.communitycare.co.uk/2018/02/14/approved-mental-health-professional-numbers-continue-decline-community-care-finds/

Collins, W. (2008) *The Woman in White.* Oxford: Oxford University Press

Cowburn, A. (2016) 'Benefit sanctions lead claimants to suicide, crime and destitution, warns damning report'. *The Independent.*

DAA News Network, (2017) 'UK: Daily Mail and Misleading Articles on Disability Benefits. Available at: http://fullfact.org/blog/disability-living-allowance-dwp-press-release-2637 (Accessed: 28.01.2019)

Davies et al. (2014) *Perceptions of Poverty. A Study of the Impact of Age on Opinions about Poverty.* University of Wales, Trinity Saint David.

Devlin, H. (2017) 'Radical new approach to schizophrenia treatment begins trial' *The Guardian*

Edmiston, D. (2016) 'Welfare, Austerity and Social Citizenship in the UK'. *Social Policy & Society 16 (2).* Doi.org/10.1017/S1474746416000531

Ernst, S. and Maguire, M. (eds) (1987) *Living with the Sphinx. Papers from the Women's Therapy Centre.* London. The Women's Press.

Equality Trust (2017) https://www.equalitytrust.or.uk

Ewing, J. (2016) 'Effects of Poverty in Early Childhood Development' (Accessed: 28.01.2019) https://prezi.com/zmeoroj8ulm3/effects-of-poverty-in-early-childhood

Ferguson, A. (2016) 'The lowest of the stack': why black women are struggling with mental health'. *The Guardian*

Flanders, J. (2014) 'Prostitution'. Discovering Literature: Romantics & Victorians. *British Library.* Available at: https://www.bl.uk/romantics-and-victorians/articles/prostitution (Accessed 07.02.2019)

Fowler, S. (2014) *The Workhouse.* Pen & Sword Books Ltd, England

Gaventa, J. (2003) 'Power after Lukes: An overview of theories of power since Lukes and their application to development'. Available at: https://www.powercube.net

Gilligan, J. (2000) *Violence. Reflections on Our Deadliest Epidemic.* London. Jessica Kingsley Publishers.

Goffman, E. (1961) *Asylums, Essays on the Social Situation of Mental Patients and Other Inmates.* Anchor

Hawken, S. (2014) 'What it's like to live with Bipolar II disorder' *The Telegraph*

Haynes, A. (1954) 'Medical Certificates Under The Lunacy and Mental Treatment Acts'. *The Lancet,* 263 (6810),p.509-511

Hewitt, D. (2011) *The nearest relative Handbook* (2nd edition), London. Jessica Kingsley Publishers

Hughes, K. et al (2018) 'The effect of multiple adverse childhood experiences on health: a systematic review and meta-analysis', *The Lancet,* 2 (8) pp.1-13 https://www.thelancet.com/journals/lanpub/article/PIIS2468-2667(17)30118-4

Hunt, M. et al, (1998) *Central Hospital Remembered.* South Warwickshire Mental Health Services NHS Trust

Hutchinson, S. (2016) 'Mental Health budgets still being cut despite pledge'. BBC. https://www.bbc.co.uk/news

Jay, M. (2016) *This Way Madness Lies.* The Asylum and Beyond. London. Thames & Hudson

Jones, R. (2011) *Mental Health Act Manual.* 14th Ed. Thomson Reuters

Joseph Rowntree Foundation (2017) 'Universal Credit: a briefing'. Available at: https://www.jrf.org.uk/report/universal-credit-briefing

Knott, G. and Bannigan, K. (2013) British Journal of Occupational Therapy, 76(3), (Accessed 28.01.2019) https://www.scie-socialcareonline.org.uk/a-critical-review-of-the-approved-mental-health-professional-role-and-occupational-therapy/r/a1CG0000001yCEGMA2

Leclerc, V. (2014) 'I had postpartum psychosis. More must be done to help mothers like me.' *The Guardian.* (Accessed: 10.12.2014) https://www.theguardian.com/commentis free/2014/dec/10/postpartum-psychosis-mothers-postnatal-depression-baby

Mariani, M. (2017) 'The neuroscience of inequality: does poverty show up in children's brains?'. *The Guardian*

Marsh, S. (2017) 'Half of children needing summer food bank support are in primary school'. *The Guardian*

Marsh, S. (2018) 'NHS patients having to be sectioned to get help, says regulator'. *The Guardian*

Maslow, A. (1954) *Motivation and Personality.* Harper.

Mayhew, H. (2012) *London Labour and the London Poor.* Oxford World's Classics

Moorhead, J. (2015) 'The Victorian women forced to give up their babies.' *The Guardian.*

Morrison,T. (2017) *The Origin of Others.* London, England. Harvard University Press

Mulholland, H. (2017) 'Jacqui Dyer: Talking about race and mental health is everyone's business'. *The Guardian*

National Health Service (2019) *Your Pregnancy and Baby Guide* Available at: https://www.nhs.uk/cnditions/pregnancy-and-baby/maternity-paternity-leave-benefits/#benefits-for-pregnant -women (Accessed:19.03.2019)

Paton, M. (2012) 'Sin and the single mother: The history of lone parenthood'. *Independent*

Picard, L. (2009) *The Great Exhibition.* Available at: https://www.bl.uk/victorian-britain/articles/the-great-exhibition. (Accessed: 07.02.2019).

Platt, S. (2017) 'Suicide in men: what is the problem?' *Trends Urology & Men's Health,* 8(4)

Press Association. (2018)''No-frills' lifestyle out of reach of parents on minimum wage – study'. *The Guardian.* Available at: https://www.theguardian.com/society/2018/20/aug/no-frills-lifestyle

Rankin, J. (2017) 'Amazon ordered to repay 250 Euros by EU over 'illegal tax advantages''. *The Guardian*

rcpsych, (2019) 'Postpartum Psychosis' Available at: https://www.rcpsych.ac.uk/healthadvice/problemsdisorders/postpartumpsychosis.aspx? (Accessed: 07.02.2019)

Rogers, A. and Pilgrim, D. (2014) *A Sociology of Mental Health and Illness.* (5th ed.) McGraw Hill Education. Open University Press

Rollins, H. (2003) 'Psychiatry in Britain one hundred years ago.' *BJPsych*, 183, pp292-298. http;//bjp.rcpsych.org.

Samaritans, (2018) 'Suicide: Facts and Figures'. Available at: 05.02.2019) https://www.samaritans.org/about-us/our-research/facts-and-figures-about-suicide (Accessed: 05.02.2019)

Samaritans, (2018) 'Suicide Statistics Report'. Samaritans.org

Scull, A. (1993) *The Most Solitary of Afflictions.* New Haven and London. Yale University Press

Showalter, E. (2004) *The Female Malady.* London. Virago

Siddique, H. (2016) 'The postcode lottery of new mothers' mental health services'. *The Guardian*

Smith, M. (2015) 'Only Connect' 'nearest relative's' experiences of mental health act assessments. *Journal of Social Work Practice.* 29:3, 339-353, DOI: 10.1080/02650533.2015.1057802

Staff reporter. (2013) 'Benefits in Britain: separating the facts from the fiction'. *The Guardian.*

Stonewall (2019) 'LGBT in Britain Health Report'. Available at: https://www.stonewall.org.uk/about us/media-releases/stonewall-report-reveals-impact-discrimination-health-lgbt-people. (Accessed: 04.03.2019).

Tew, J. (2011) *Social Approaches to mental distress.* Palgrave Macmillan

The Guardian, (2013) '*Benefits in Britain: separating the facts from the fiction*'. Available at: https://www.theguardian.com/politics/2013/apr/06/welfare-britain-facts-myths

The Money Advice Service. Available at: https://www.moneyadviceservice.org.uk

The Office of National Statistics (ONS). Available at: https://www.ons.gov.uk (Accessed: 05.02.2019)

Thompson, T. and Mathias, P. (Eds) (2003*) Lyttles' Mental Health and Disorder.* Bailliere Tindall

Twenge, J. (2018) 'Are Smartphones causing more teen suicides?' *The Guardian.* https://www.theguardian.com/society/2018/may/24

Usborne, S. (2017) 'The bold new fight to eradicate suicide'. *The Guardian. https://www.theguardian.com/society/2017/aug/01/zero-suicide-the-bold-new-fight-to-eradicate-suicide?*

White, J. (2008) *London in the 19th Century.* Great Britain. Vintage

Winnicott, D. (2006) *The Family and Individual Development.* London and New York. Routledge Classics.

Winnicott, D. (2007) *The Maturational Processes and the Facilitating Environment.* London. Karnac Books.

Wise, S. (2013*) Inconvenient People, Lunacy, Liberty and the Mad-doctors in Victorian England*. London. Vintage.

Worsley, L. (2013) 'What was the truth about the madness of George lll?' *BBC News.* Available at: https://www.bbc.co.uk/news/magazine-22122407. Accessed: 30.04.2019